AURA GARDEN GUIDES

Colin Lewis

Bonsai Basics

Practical advice on choosing and
caring for bonsai trees

AURA BOOKS

Aura Garden Guides

Bonsai Basics
Colin Lewis

© 2002 Advanced Marketing (UK) Ltd.,
Bicester, England

Produced by:
Transedition Limited for
Aura Books, Bicester
and first published in 2002

Editing by:
Asgard Publishing Services, Leeds

Typesetting by:
Organ Graphic, Abingdon

Picture Credits
All photographs by the author
except the following:
Herons 7, 36–7; Bill Jordan 2–3, 5,
12, 13, 21, 22, 23, 57, 62, 63, 64,
66, 67, 69, 73, 78–9.

All drawings by Colin Fargher,
Fargher Design, Douglas, Isle of Man.

10 9 8 7 6 5 4 3 2
Printed in Dubai

ISBN 1 901683 04 4

Colin Lewis has been growing bonsai for almost 30 years and has gained an international reputation as an artist and author.

He teaches regularly throughout the UK, Europe and the United States and in 2001 was awarded second prize in the Japan Airlines World Bonsai Contest for his work with Scots pine. This is his seventh book.

CONTENTS

A Chinese juniper grown according to the classical cascade style

Origins of bonsai

Beginnings

There are many myths and legends surrounding the precise origin of bonsai, though the full truth will never be known. My favourite is the story of an emperor who was so fat he couldn't leave his palace. He missed travelling around his domain, seeing the mountains, rivers and forests. He commanded that a scale model of his entire empire should be constructed in his courtyard, so that he could survey it from his balcony every day. I doubt it's true, but it's a nice thought.

What we can be sure of is that, while the Ancient Britons were still using bronze axes and wooden ploughs, the Chinese were busy conquering the horticultural and artistic complexities of making and keeping miniature landscapes in shallow containers. Murals painted over 3,000 years ago in emperors' tombs depict miniature trees, rocks and small grasses planted in dishes. These appear to have been valued gifts — so valued that their images accompanied the emperors to the hereafter.

Some 2,000 years later, around the time Robin Hood was robbing the rich, the Chinese exerted a vast cultural influence across most of the Far East, including Japan, where many aspects of Chinese culture became forever ingrained in Japanese life. Among these was bonsai.

Japanese influence

It was inevitable that the Japanese, being such a dedicated and disciplined society, would refine both the horticultural and aesthetic aspects of bonsai to the level of a fine art. The spiritual aspect of bonsai wasn't neglected either. For a period during the 17th century, bonsai was considered to be so intensely spiritual that only holy men or the topmost nobility were allowed to own them. This was followed by alternating periods of near-obscurity and high artistic

profile until the late 19th century, when bonsai finally became a part of everyday life in Japan.

Ironically, only 20 years or so after bonsai had become established in popular culture, all knowledge of it was almost wiped out by a devastating earthquake that destroyed the main bonsai-growing areas in northern Japan. Few masters survived. Those who did moved south to Omiya, a small village outside Tokyo, where they started afresh as a co-operative. Omiya village is now a suburb of Tokyo, but most of the original nurseries are still there and being run by the descendants of that original band.

Another two decades later, Japan suffered yet more disaster. The havoc wrought by the 2nd World War, and the horrific results of the two atomic bombs dropped by allied forces, destroyed vast numbers of ancient masterpieces as well as many of the new growing grounds. Even this heartbreaking period, coming so soon after the earthquake, failed to break the Japanese bonsai masters' resolve. Such is the dedication that grips the confirmed bonsai addict.

Moving west

Ironically, it was the Western occupying forces returning from Japan who were largely responsible for introducing bonsai to the West on a popular level. There had been a few attempts to import these 'mysterious Japanese trees' to Britain and France around the 1900s, but in the absence of any knowledge of their upkeep, none had survived long. However, after the war, the ex-patriot Japanese community living in America was only too keen to start spreading the word. Soon there were books, classes and eventually clubs springing up here and there.

The first club in Britain was formed in the early 1960s, and it is still going strong today — along with about 90 or so others. Today there are magazines, several annual exhibitions,

Perfect specimens like this 40-year-old Korean hornbeam are the culmination of a centuries-old tradition of growing trees in small pots.

conventions and professional teachers offering courses and workshops. Small, starter bonsai are seen in garden centres, hardware stores, market stalls and, at Christmas time, even on garage forecourts. Almost everybody has seen or heard about bonsai, but only relatively few know how to care for them. After reading this book, you should be one of them.

What makes a bonsai?

Some myths dispelled

In simple terms, a bonsai is just a tree in a pot — which is more or less literally what the Japanese word *bonsai* means. But literal translations seldom get the whole message across. Try, for example, translating egg-timer into Japanese and they will find this hilarious: 'Time an egg! Doing what?' The wealth of cultural symbolism that surrounds the image of such a simple everyday tool is lost.

To be more specific, a bonsai is a miniature representation of a full-grown tree — real or imaginary — cultivated in an aesthetically compatible container.

Any species of tree has the potential to be cultivated as a bonsai, although some are better than others. A common misconception is that dwarf varieties make the best bonsai, whereas this is not often the case. Genetically dwarfed plants are weak growers and more susceptible to disease. Trees with naturally large or compound leaves, like chestnut and ash, are also

difficult. Their foliage will reduce after many years in bonsai cultivation, but never enough to match the scale of the tree. Trees such as beech, hawthorn, pine, larch and elm make fine bonsai, as do many garden shrubs, such as Chinese juniper, azalea, quince, cotoneaster and more.

Another misconception is that bonsai are kept small by the application of some magic potion, or by withholding nutrients. Some people compare growing a tree in a pot to the long-abandoned practice of binding Chinese women's feet to keep them small. Nothing could be further from the truth. Bonsai are probably among the best cared-for plants in cultivation. If bonsai weren't maintained in excellent health, they would never reach the staggering age that they do, even outliving their full-size counterparts.

Buying bonsai

Developing your own bonsai takes time and a great deal of discipline: daily watering in summer, regular feeding and trimming, annual repotting, wire-training and, of course, unwiring. Understandably, most people prefer to get a head start by buying their first bonsai or two, so they have something to appreciate and for learning the techniques on — and why not?

Always remember that you're buying a living thing. What's more, it has been developed in another climate and shipped halfway round the world in a dark container before reaching the store or nursery. Any plant would need a period of recovery after such an ordeal, but not all bonsai get this — or at least to a sufficient extent. As with most things, you get what you

The larch makes an excellent candidate for bonsai. This specimen has been grown in the classical root-over-rock style.

pay for. If you buy a cheap bonsai from a market stall or supermarket, you shouldn't be too surprised if it is dead within a couple of weeks. You might assume that you're no good with bonsai, or that bonsai simply die on you — but it wouldn't be your fault.

The best places to buy bonsai are specialist nurseries, whose livelihoods depend on good products and service. If there isn't one near you, look for a reputable garden centre where the staff will be knowledgeable about plants in general, and will have properly cared for the stock in their possession.

What to buy

There are three major criteria to consider when buying bonsai. First you must like the way it looks. Whether or not its appearance takes your fancy is an entirely personal matter, but as you become more discerning, your tastes will tend towards a more tree-like appearance than some commercial bonsai.

Herons of East Grinstead is a good example of a specialist bonsai nursery. Bonsai from such establishments don't come cheap, but you can be sure they have been properly looked after.

The other two criteria are more scientific. The second major factor is the matter of the plant's health. The health of any plant can usually be detected in the foliage. Lush, green, blemish-free leaves usually indicate a healthy tree. Yellowing leaves, old as well as new, indicate over-watering or a nutrient deficiency. Brown foliage is dead — and if that part of a tree is dead, the rest might soon follow. Gently test the trunk to see if the tree is stable in the pot. If it wobbles easily, the root system is poor and the tree will therefore be weak.

The third consideration is where you intend to keep the tree — indoors or outdoors? For detailed advice on this, turn to page 12.

The anatomy of a tree

All higher plants have thee main components: roots, stems (trunks and branches in the case of trees) and leaves. Each of these components performs a specific function and has specific requirements if it is to perform that function efficiently.

Roots

The first function of roots is structural: they anchor the tree in the ground. Unhealthy roots are weak. Weak-rooted trees rock in strong winds, which causes further root damage, leading to an early demise.

The second function of roots is to gather moisture, together with water-borne nutrients and minerals, from the soil. To do this, they spread out in all directions and issue fine feeding roots covered in root hairs. The walls of the root hairs provide the surface through which the water and nutrients pass into the root in a process called osmosis. The more feeding roots a tree can produce, the stronger and healthier it will be.

In our climate, roots only grow in spring and summer. Every autumn and winter, most of the previous summer's feeding roots will die back, to be replaced by fresh new roots the following spring. The few roots that survive the winter

will thicken in spring and sprout their own set of new feeding roots. They will then become connecting roots, transporting water and nutrients towards the trunk.

Clearly, in a small bonsai container, this cycle can only be repeated for a couple of seasons before the pot becomes completely filled with thickening roots, leaving no room for fresh feeder roots to grow. We get around this problem by pruning the roots periodically (see pages 41–3). Not only is this harmless to the tree, but it is of enormous benefit.

A third function of roots is winter storage of sugars. By late summer, a healthy tree will be brimming with energy-giving sugars that the foliage has been producing since spring. Thick, woody roots serve as storage compartments for many of the excess sugars. As the soil warms in spring, the sugars are released to provide energy for new root and foliage growth.

Trunk and branches

The first function of the trunk and branches is structural. They support the foliage at a height and spread that enables the leaves to gather the maximum possible light.

The second function is to transport water and nutrients from the roots to the shoots and

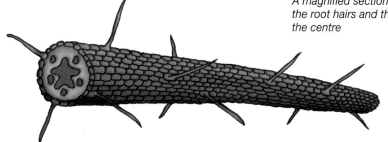

A magnified section of a root tip showing the root hairs and the transport vessels in the centre

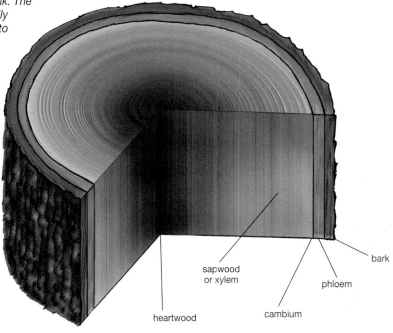

Cross section of a trunk. The heartwood is essentially dead and serves only to strengthen the trunk.

sapwood or xylem

bark

phloem

heartwood

cambium

leaves, and to carry the sugars produced by the leaves to their storage areas or to locations where growth energy is needed.

The central core — the *heartwood* — of the trunk and heavy branches is dead. Its only function is to add physical strength. The outer bark is also dead. Its function is to waterproof the tree and to provide protection from physical damage.

Water and nutrients are transported upward through the outer few annual rings — the *sapwood* or *xylem*. Sugars are transported back down the branches and trunk through the living inner bark — the *phloem*.

Between the xylem and the phloem is a single-cell layer called the *cambium*, which shows green if you scratch the bark of a twig. This is where it all happens! During the growing season the cambium cells are constantly dividing, producing new xylem on the inside and

new phloem on the outside. This accounts for the familiar annual rings in a trunk. The cambium is also responsible for creating new roots after root pruning, and new buds on old branches, as well as the healing callus that forms on wounds.

Like the roots, the trunk also performs a winter storage function. Sugars are stored in compartments called medullary rays that radiate from the core toward the sapwood. The sugars stored here are mainly used for new foliage growth. However, some are retained in case of emergencies.

Foliage

Foliage can be considered to be made up of three elements: buds, shoots and leaves. Let's look at them in chronological order, starting the story in spring.

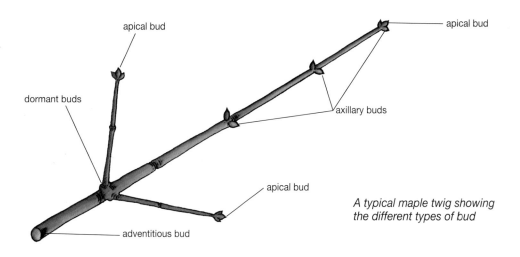

apical bud

apical bud

dormant buds

axillary buds

apical bud

*A typical maple twig showing
the different types of bud*

adventitious bud

Buds

Just to complicate matters, buds come in three types: primary, dormant and adventitious.

First there are *primary* or *apical buds* — nice fat ones that form on recent growth. These will open in spring and sprout new shoots and leaves. Primary buds are formed at the junction of the leaf stalk (petiole) and the shoot.

On deciduous trees, every leaf will have a bud at the base of its petiole. Conifers only have buds at the base of random needles. The number of these buds is dependent on the health and vigour of the tree.

Then there are *dormant buds*, which were once primary buds but lacked the energy to open. They can remain viable for many years, waiting to be prompted into growth by pruning or the thinning of dense foliage.

Finally there are *adventitious buds*. These buds are generated by the cambium and spring out from beneath the bark on older branches and even the trunk. Adventitious buds are usually prompted by pruning or damage. A very old, weather-beaten tree will sometimes begin to sprout adventitious growth from the base of the trunk in a last-ditch attempt at survival.

All buds, no matter how small, are tightly packed kits containing everything required for a new shoot, all wrapped up in scales (which are, themselves, modified leaves). Think of a Brussels sprout (which is a giant bud) cut in half to reveal its structure. Now reduce that to the size of a Chinese elm or serissa bud — half the size of a pinhead!

*A magnified cross-section of a
typical broadleaved bud. Note
how it contains all the features of
the potential shoot in minute detail.*

Shoots

Shoots are essential for spacing the leaves to allow them all to receive light, and for extending the tree year by year. The outer shoots are most vigorous because they receive more light, and they are destined to become future branches as the tree grows. Inner shoots don't grow so much — sometimes hardly at all. They survive as a back-up facility in case the outer leaves are damaged by weather or insects. If the outer leaves or shoots are pruned away, the inner shoots will become more vigorous.

Leaves

The structure and appearance of leaves varies enormously between species, from wide, flat sycamore leaves through complex shapes like acacia to the tiny needles on spruce and juniper. Some have waxy coatings to prevent evaporation in hot sun. Others have hairy surfaces which perform a similar service. Some are red, others variegated green and yellow, but all perform one essential function.

Leaves are food factories, using water from the roots, carbon dioxide from the air and light from the sun to manufacture sugars in a process called *photosynthesis*. The green pigment in leaves, the *chlorophyll*, provides the wherewithal for photosynthesis to take place. All leaves have pores that inhale air and exhale water vapour, oxygen and other waste gasses.

 Understanding bonsai

A bonsai is a living tree, no different from the giants we see around us in parks and in the countryside. If taken from its pot and planted in the open ground, it will eventually grow into a full-size specimen.

Life in a pot is not a natural state for any plant, let alone a tree, so it is essential to balance the restriction of the roots with an equal restriction of the growth of twigs and foliage. Understanding how a tree works — how it grows, regenerates and eventually grows old — can help us achieve these goals.

If properly cared for, a bonsai will never actually reach full maturity — it will always remain juvenile and will outlive its current and possibly even its future owners.

A section of a typical leaf (greatly magnified)

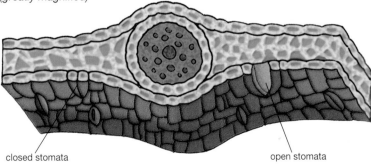

closed stomata

open stomata

Indoors or outdoors?

First, there is no such thing as an indoor tree! All trees are designed to live outside in the fresh air where they receive sun, wind and rain. Having said that, modern homes can provide suitable conditions for some subtropical and tropical species. This is just as well, since people are increasingly living in cities, where they have little or no outside space.

Indoors
Most houseplants are subtropical in origin, so if you can keep those healthy, you should have no problem with subtropical bonsai. But if you do keep subtropical bonsai, they will benefit tremendously from being introduced to the open air when the weather is warm enough. There's something about fresh air, natural filtered sunlight and gentle rain — the tree seems to know. The colour will improve, the growth will become sturdier, and it will look much happier in general appearance. If you don't have a garden or balcony, even a windowsill will do, so long as the tree isn't left in the blazing sun all day until it has fully acclimatised.

Tropical species may need a little more heat, and especially humidity, than you would find comfortable in your living room. The real tropical bonsai enthusiast will go to great expense to build a temperature and humidity-controlled conservatory. Fortunately, there are few truly tropical species in commercial bonsai production.

Outdoors
If you don't want to clutter your home with bonsai, or if you're a confirmed bonsai addict, your garden will soon be overrun with hardy bonsai. These will not tolerate indoor conditions at any time of year. Hardy species can tolerate

The Japanese white pine is a species that will only grow well out of doors.

Outdoor bonsai can be brought indoors for display purposes, but they are kept there too long they will soon deteriorate.

freezing of the soil in the pot for several days or longer. Many of them absolutely must have a period of freezing in order to remain healthy — or even to survive.

They can be brought indoors for display for a few days, but must soon be returned to their natural habitat. If they're kept inside for too long in summer, the shoots will become very long and spindly, and will eventually collapse and die. If they're kept indoors for more

than a day or so in winter, their natural and necessary period of dormancy may be broken and all the primary buds will be lost. This can sometimes even be fatal!

The following rules of thumb are worth remembering:

• All conifers (pine, spruce, juniper, yew, cedar, larch, cypress) are fully hardy and cannot live indoors.

• All broadleaved deciduous species (maple, beech, horn-beam, apple, apricot, cherry) are fully hardy and cannot live indoors.

• Elms and zelkovas are often wrongly named in order to

circumvent the import regula-tions. If you're in any doubt about their identity, then if they're Japanese they're fully hardy, but if they're not Japanese they're more than likely subtropical.

• If you're in really serious doubt, buy your bonsai in winter. If it's on display in full growth in a greenhouse, you can be certain it's a subtropical or tropical species. If it's displayed outside, it's hardy — or dead! To check, scratch the bark with your fingernail, discreet-ly, on the underside of a branch. If you see green (the cambium), it's alive.

13

Water

Water is fundamental to all plant life. Without water a tree will die — in a bone-dry bonsai container, a tree will die of thirst within as little as 48 hours.

That's where most newcomers make their first mistake. More bonsai are killed through panic over-watering than any other cause — possibly more than all the other causes combined.

When to water

The first and only rule to learn is this:

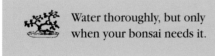 Water thoroughly, but only when your bonsai needs it.

The real question is, how can you tell? The answer is simple: healthy roots colonise the entire pot — apart from a thin surface layer in some cases — which means that the soil dries fairly uniformly throughout the pot.

 Scratch test

Scratch the dry surface to expose the soil immediately below:

• If the soil just below the surface is clearly wet, your tree doesn't need watering yet.
• If it is damp, you *can* water.
• If it is dry, you *must* water.

After a few weeks, you should be able to judge reasonably accurately just by looking at the surface of the soil. Besides, too much scratching

away at the surface of the soil will compact the roots, so if you are still unsure of your judgement, try this simple test:

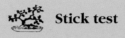 **Stick test**

• Insert a wooden stick (e.g. a chopstick or kebab stick) into the soil in one corner of the pot.
• Push it right to the floor of the pot and leave it there.
• Withdraw it every day and feel the end. This will tell you exactly how damp the soil is at all levels.

How to water

This might sound obvious, but by far the best way to water is from above, using a fine rose on a watering can. This needs to be said, though, because there are so many silly myths about watering bonsai by plunging them up to their necks in the bathtub every day.

Some imported subtropical trees arrive in this country planted in a heavy, grey clay-like soil, which is fine for the humidity of Taiwan but useless in the much drier atmosphere of your your home. These may need to be dunked in a bowl of water once a week or so to ensure the soil gets a good soaking. But they should be replanted using a better soil at the earliest appropriate opportunity (see page 36ff.).

What water?

Another strange question, perhaps, but you'd be surprised how many people buy bottled water for their bonsai. If tap water doesn't harm people, it won't harm bonsai. Nowadays, rain-water in some areas contains more impurities than tap water. Bottled water is just an unnecessary expense.

The only exceptions to this are lime-hating species such as azaleas, which need an acid soil. If you live in a hard water area, they will need regular applications of a soil acidifier such as Miracid.

The perils of over-watering

Over-watering is the biggest killer of bonsai. Excess water can literally drown the roots. The dead roots rot in the soggy soil and the decay enters thicker, live roots, thwarting all the tree's efforts to produce new roots.

Whereas drought can kill a bonsai in just a day or two, over-watering is a more subtle killer. It

can take weeks or even months for the damage to become apparent, by which time it's usually too late to save the tree.

Since rotting roots can't absorb any water, the tree begins to suffer symptoms of drought. The leaves lose colour and wilt, and you start to panic, thinking that wilting leaves mean that even more water is needed — and so the problem is compounded.

If you think you've been over-watering and your bonsai is looking a bit sad, try the remedy shown below. Lift the tree out of its pot — gently, mind — and plant it in a larger container, surrounding the intact root ball with dry sand. Use the stick test described opposite to see when the soil is beginning to dry out, and only water sparingly at first. Don't feed the tree until it has fully recovered.

How to dry out waterlogged roots
The undisturbed root ball is planted in a large, well-drained container, surrounded by coarse sand.

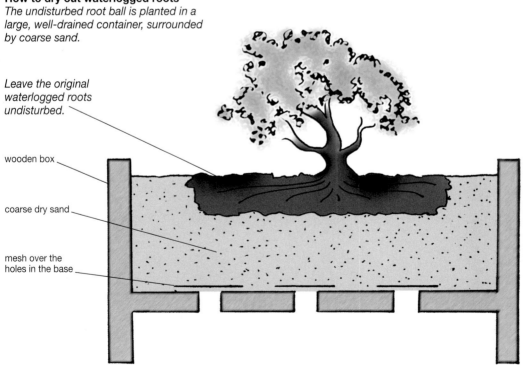

Leave the original waterlogged roots undisturbed.

wooden box

coarse dry sand

mesh over the holes in the base

Nutrition

Bonsai soil is largely inert, containing little or nothing of nutritional value to a tree. What nutrients may exist there are soon washed away with daily watering. This means your bonsai is entirely dependent on you for its nutritional requirements.

Which to use?

There is a bewildering array of plant foods available, all of them claiming to be best for one thing or another. Yet the truth is that the basic ingredients are all much the same, although the proportions may vary. The proportions of the three basic nutrients — nitrogen (N), phosphorus (P) and potassium (K) — are more important than brand name or the type of fertiliser (solid, liquid etc.).

Somewhere on the pack of every fertiliser will be the initials NPK followed by three numbers. This indicates the relative proportions of the three basic nutrients. For example, NPK 15-15-15 indicates a balanced feed of medium strength; NPK 30-10-10 means high in nitrogen; NPK 5-6-6 shows a balanced feed of low strength, and so on.

So just what does all this mean in practice? Let's look at the three nutrients in turn, and see how the tree uses them.

Nitrogen (N)

Nitrogen is responsible for leaf and stem growth. With too little nitrogen, the leaves become pale, while the stems are thin and weak, and both become susceptible to fungal disease. If there's no nitrogen at all, eventually the stem and leaves collapse and the plant will die.

Plants that consist predominantly of foliage — such as grass, cabbage and many houseplants — require nitrogen in high quantities. Trees, however, are more complex structures and will generally prefer a more balanced diet.

The Japanese azalea (far left) produces a magnificent display of flowers. Azaleas, like other lime-hating plants, require an acid soil, so if you live in a hard water area they will need regular applications of a soil acidifier (see page 15).

In open ground, decaying organisms are a prime source of phosphorus.

Potassium (K)

Potassium (potash) plays a balancing act with the nitrogen. It hardens off the young growth and protects it against fungal attack and cold damage

Too little potash can result in mottled foliage, 'burning' of the leaf margins and premature autumn leaf fall.

Gardeners spread bonfire ash around their perennials to increase the potash in the soil.

What NPK?

The proportion of nutrients to use will depend on the time of year. In spring a weak balanced feed is all your tree will need — something in the region of 5-5-5. Then, as the shoots begin to extend, the tree's nutrient requirements will increase, so the strength can be increased to, say, 15-15-15 or thereabouts. Toward the end of summer and through early autumn, a nitrogen-free

Nitrogen is naturally produced in the open ground as a result of decaying plant matter and is topped up by animal waste. Farm manure is a rich source of nitrogen for the garden, but far too potent for bonsai.

Phosphorus (P)

Phosphorus takes care of root development and also helps the ripening of fruit. The latter is especially important in the case of bonsai which have berries, such as cotoneaster and Japanese holly (*Ilex serrata*).

Insufficient phosphorus results in poor root growth, and this in turn is reflected in the formation of small, purple-tinted leaves.

fertiliser such as 0-10-10 helps to harden off the buds and roots in readiness for winter.

The one major exception to this rule is the pine family. Pines need a low-nitrogen diet in spring and early summer, followed by high nitrogen in late summer, in order to build buds for next year.

For tropical and subtropical bonsai growing indoors, a gentle winter feed at half strength will keep them healthy during their period of reduced or non-existent growth. But having said all that, if you use your usual houseplant fertiliser as instructed on the pack, you won't go far wrong.

This solid organic fertiliser provides some extra benefits in the form of micro-organisms and a few trace elements. The granules release the nutrients slowly into the soil over a long period.

Trace elements

In addition to the three main nutrients, plants also need a variety of other chemicals, but in minute quantities. Most commercial fertilisers also contain trace elements, but it's worth checking before you buy.

The two most important trace elements are magnesium and iron. Magnesium is responsible for the production of chlorophyll, without which the leaves become yellow between the veins and can no longer manufacture life-giving sugars. Iron is thought to help in the tree's distribution system. A deficiency results in yellowing veins on the leaves and generally weak growth.

Organic or synthetic?

There's a lot of talk these days about the benefits of organic growing methods. To be honest, trees don't know or care what they get their nutrients from. They are equally as happy with

factory-produced chemicals as with a nice lump of well-rotted manure.

However, organic fertilisers do contain some (though seldom many) trace elements and, more important, lots of lovely micro-organisms. These are necessary to help the organic matter break down and release its nutrients. They also turn the soil into a living environment for the roots to flourish in.

Liquid or solid?

Here there is a real choice to be made, based on personal preference and discipline.

Liquid feeds are more efficient in the short term because the nutrients are immediately available to the roots. However, in a bonsai pot they're not available for long because daily watering soon leaches them from the soil. Regular disciplined applications are necessary, and you should always follow the manufacturer's instructions.

Solid fertilisers, whether organic or synthetic, are slow-release granules that degrade slowly and make their nutrients available to the plant over a period of time. With solid fertilisers you wash nutrients into the soil whenever you water. Most, though, require warm temperatures to function properly, so very early spring feeds are a waste of time.

I personally use a combination of solid organic and liquid synthetic feeds. I give a dose of organic NPK 6-6-6 in spring and again in midsummer. Between times, I top up with a few applications of liquid chemical fertiliser of an appropriate formula. This has worked very well for the last 20 years or so.

 Killing with kindness

Too much fertiliser can be fatal, so don't think you're doing your tree a favour by doubling the dose.

If the concentration of nutrient salts in the soil is too strong, water will be drawn out of the roots and back into the soil by reverse osmosis, killing the roots and probably the tree too.

Remember that you're growing a miniature tree, not a prize marrow!

 Organic v. inorganic

There have always been arguments within horticultural circles about the relative merits of organic versus inorganic (or synthetic) fertilisers.

But the fact is that a tree neither knows nor cares where its nutrients come from — whether from decaying organic matter or from a factory-produced compound in a bottle. Just so long as the tree receives the correct nutrients in reasonable quantities, it will grow away perfectly happily.

The most important thing to remember is not to try to second-guess the manufacturers. Always use products exactly as directed on the package and you won't have any problems at all.

Light and air

Light

Daylight — or a good artificial substitute — is essential for plant survival. But it is important to understand the difference between sunlight and sunshine. Direct sunlight can be too harsh for many species, especially through the glass window of your living room. All bonsai, whether indoors or out, will benefit from some degree of dappled shading from the hot summer sun — even in the UK.

If you keep indoor bonsai, you should place them near enough to a large window so that they receive good light, but not where the sun will shine directly on them. Moreover, if you take your indoor bonsai seriously, it's worth investing in some horticultural growing lights to supplement the poor light during the colder half of the year.

In the case of outdoor bonsai, maple, beech and larch are the worst affected by strong sun — they will need semi-shade for certain. At the opposite end of the spectrum, pines will be delighted to bake away all day long in full sun. Fortunately, pines are fairly drought-tolerant, so when the pot dries through evaporation, no damage will be done to the tree — provided you water it

The ideal placement for indoor bonsai. Make sure that the tree receives good light but not direct sun all day.

before the next day. You don't have to keep pines in full sun, but you can if you want to.

Ventilation

There's air all a round us, so what's the problem? Yes, but is it circulating? You know how it feels when you step out of a stuffy room into the fresh air. Well, your trees feel the same way. Stagnant air breeds mildew and other nasty fungal problems, disrupts the tree's natural 'breathing' rhythm and generally makes bonsai look dowdy. Try to provide a change of air in the room every

hour or so whenever you're at home. If necessary, a small fan would be useful.

Even outdoors, trees that are packed close together, three rows deep on their display benches, will also be sitting in pretty stagnant air. Some foliage will be lost, and lower and inner branches may die. Many insect pests also prefer the clandestine environment amongst the congested branches. The other problem is that if your trees are too closely packed, you may not see any problems until it's too late to remedy them.

Pests and diseases

Insect pests

Bonsai are susceptible to precisely the same pests that attack other plants in your home or garden. However, unlike free-growing plants, bonsai are unable to outgrow infestations.

Fortunately, the high season for pests coincides with the high season for watering, so you will be visiting each tree at least once a day. Take a little time to examine them closely, looking for signs of pests.

Bonsai are no different from other plants when it comes to the treament of pests. Ordinary garden remedies can be used, though you should be careful you follow the manufacturers' instructions.

The familiar greenfly is among the commonest of the many garden pests.

Aphids

Symptoms: leaves emerging from the shoot tip distorted; some recent leaves curling.

Aphids tend to lurk underneath the leaves or along the very tip of the shoot. Look closely, because many aphids adopt the colour of the leaf or shoot they're feeding on. Destroy any nearby ants' nests, because the ants will quickly re-introduce aphids from elsewhere.

Mildew, like other fungal diseases, is most often caused by poor ventilation. If you want to avoid it, allow plenty of air to circulate around your plants.

The spider mite, here greatly magnified, is practically invisible to the naked eye. An infestation will be apparent from the damage caused to the plant.

Spider mites

Symptoms: patches of dry foliage, particularly on small-needled conifers. Some fine, web-like structures may be seen, but the mites are too small to be seen with the naked eye. Try gently shaking the affected branch over a piece of white paper. If tiny black specs appear, these are dead spider mites. The live ones cling on tight.

Caterpillars are attractive to look at and don't do much harm, but are best removed.

Caterpillars

Symptoms: large holes in leaves, usually at the edges.

Caterpillars are harmless really, unless they are present in large numbers. Always look under the all leaves, and not just those with holes in. Remove them by hand.

Vine weevils

Symptoms: 3–4-mm diameter holes in the edges of the leaves of some species, particularly azaleas, indicate the presence of adult vine weevils.

The adult weevils are harmless in themselves, but if they're present you can be sure they have laid eggs in your pot. The larvae from one clutch of eggs could devour an entire root system within a few weeks. The first you will know about it is when the leaves suddenly wilt for no apparent reason. By then it's too late.

Protection is therefore the best policy. The weevils can't fly, so by placing the pots on stones in a tray of water, or wrapping grease bands round the legs of the display benches, you can stop them reaching your trees.

In cases where an infestation has already occurred, chemical treatments are now available to

The adult vine weevil is a small beetle that is harmless in itself, but its larvae can do untold damage to a plant. Prevention is therefore better than cure.

the amateur gardener, but they need to be used precisely as instructed, both for your own safety and for that of the tree.

Diseases

Fungal diseases are unsightly on plants, but on bonsai they rarely prove fatal.

Here again, normal garden treatments are appropriate. Most packs have illustrations of the types of fungus they will treat, and all of them have very detailed instructions, which must be followed.

Pine needle cast can be fatal to pines but is fortunately treatable.

Pine needle cast

One disease that is unfamiliar to the gardener can be fatal to pines — namely needle cast.

Yellow patches appear on the needles, with tiny brown pustules in the middle. The needles turn quite quickly yellow and fall.

Fortunately, a good copper-based fungicide, applied at regular intervals all summer, will clear the infection.

Tools and equipment

Cutting tools

To begin with, you can make do with ordinary household tools such as nail scissors, secateurs, modelling knife etc. If you only have one or two trees, you can manage with improvised tools for as long as you like. But if you become a true bonsai hobbyist, you'll want to build your own set of bonsai tools.

Where bonsai tools are concerned, buying the cheapest is certainly a false economy. Bonsai tools are expensive at the best of times, so cheap ones are rarely very cheap and the poor quality will disappoint you. Look for brand-marked Japanese tools — nothing fancy, just plain black. Looked after properly, they'll last a lifetime.

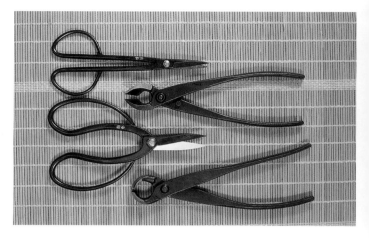

The table below lists all the tools according to how frequently they are used, to indicate which ones you're recommended to buy first. By the time you've acquired that lot, you will already have decided what's next.

A selection of bonsai tools — from top of bottom: medium twig shears, a side cutter, root shears and a concave cutter

Wire

You can try salvaging some copper wire from electrical or telephone cables, then annealing it by heating it to red hot and allowing it to cool slowly — and then you'll need to wash off the soot. On the other hand, while you're spending money on tools, you might as well pick up some wire at the same time.

Wire is used for shaping branches (see page 46), and for this ordinary garden wire — green-plastic-coated iron — is far too rigid and is sure to damage the bark when you apply it. Traditionally, either

Types of bonsai cutter

Twig shears	available in three sizes	start with the medium size
Side cutters	available in three sizes	start with the medium size
Wire cutters	available in two sizes	start with the small size
Concave cutters	available in several sizes	start with a smallish size
Root shears	available in two sizes	start with the small size

annealed copper wire or brown anodised aluminium wire is used.

Copper hardens as it is bent, so it has greater holding power than aluminium — ideal for the springier branches of conifers. The gentler aluminium wire is kinder to the less-supple branches of deciduous trees. Having said that, aluminium is usually cheaper and works as well as copper provided you use a thicker gauge.

There are nine gauges of aluminium wire, ranging from 1 mm to 6 mm. Copper wire gauges vary from supplier to supplier, but are roughly equivalent.

To begin with, you should buy small packs of the smaller sizes. When you've worked out which sizes you need more of, go for larger coils.

Other equipment

When repotting time arrives, you'll need sieves to remove the dust and coarse particles from your soil ingredients. A set of three with mesh sizes of 2 mm, 3 mm and 4 mm will be plenty for most small and medium-size bonsai. Larger bonsai in larger pots need larger soil particles, so an additional sieve with a 6-mm mesh would be useful. A bonsai soil scoop makes life easier at this time as well.

You'll also need a bonsai root hook and some chopsticks (or a Western substitute such as knitting needles) for teasing out the roots. Japanese bonsai root hooks are a little too brutal for most trees, and the tiny rakes with tweezers at the other end are only useful for weeding the pot. My favourite

Among the most essential items for repotting bonsai are a set of seives, a root hook and a soil scoop.

root hook is one that I made from a piece of 4-mm steel rod and an old chisel handle over 20 years ago.

A turntable is invaluable for trimming, wiring or just contemplating your bonsai. There are several all-singing, all-dancing Japanese bonsai turntables available but they are very expensive. An old cake decorator's turntable or a plastic TV turntable will do just as well.

There are many more useful little gadgets you can pick up along the way, but those discussed here are the ones that, if not essential, are hard to do without.

Pruning

Doesn't it hurt the tree?

No more than pruning hurts your roses or that dusty old privet hedge that you unceremoniously hack back too many times a year. In fact, pruning an established bonsai helps keep the foliage mass in equilibrium with the roots, thus balancing the tree's needs with its ability to supply them.

Experienced gardeners will tell you that the best time to prune is autumn, but there is no evidence to support this. Pruning in autumn risks considerable die-back around the wound, from frost and water damage. The tree has to wait several months before it can begin to heal or regenerate, which must be bad news.

Traditional gardening practice is quite probably based more on the fact that in spring and summer there are more chores to do than in autumn, rather than on sound horticultural sense.

There are three reasons for pruning a bonsai:

• to encourage new vigorous shoots for developing into branches
• to reduce long branches to a more suitable length for further development
• to thin out congested areas on established bonsai.

We'll look at each one in turn.

Pruning for new growth

When developing deciduous bonsai from scratch, it's quite common the cut all the branches off flush with the trunk and use some of the new shoots that arise as a result to begin branch development. Later, when the shoots have themselves become thick and sturdy, further drastic pruning is done to generate secondary branching.

The timing of this type of pruning can have significant impact on its success. For a good crop of new adventitious buds to appear and grow away strongly, three conditions must be fulfilled. First, the tree must have plenty of energy-giving sugars in its system. Second, there must be chemical signals coming from the roots (cytokinins) to tell the area of cambium around the wound to

Developmental pruning may seem rather drastic, but new growth soon begins to form where branches have been removed.

get moving on new bud production. Both these conditions are fulfilled at almost any time during the growing season. The third condition is that there must be sufficient growing time left for the new shoots to become established and harden off before winter.

The ideal time for developmental pruning is midsummer — around the middle of June in the UK. Within two or three weeks a crown of tightly packed buds will appear between the bark and the wood at the edge of the wound. More buds will also appear from random points all over the tree.

Many of the new shoots will spontaneously abort before they become established. This is nothing to worry about — it's just the tree deciding for itself which it would prefer to retain as new branches. You should allow it to do this, then further reduce the number of shoots in autumn.

If you prune out of season — during winter or early spring — there will be fewer if any buds formed around the wound, and only a handful of new shoots growing from elsewhere.

Shortening branches
The principle behind reduction pruning is similar to that of development pruning above, but the timing is usually less crucial.

More often than not, there will be some dormant buds, or at least visible internodes, at or near the point where you want to prune back to. If this is the case, you can prune either in midsummer or in late winter or very early spring, just as the buds at the tips of the twigs start to swell.

If there are no clearly visible buds or internodes, prune in midsummer following the procedure outlined above

If you're only pruning one or two branches, you must reduce the amount of foliage on the parts of the tree above the wounds and turn the pruning cuts to face the sun. This prevents the tree from channelling all its energy towards

the upper part of the tree at the expense of the pruned branches. Trees are essentially lazy, and will always take the easy way out if you let them.

 Important
Needle conifers (e.g. pines) and scale conifers (junipers, cypresses) will never produce buds on branches that have no foliage elsewhere. Pruning away all the foliage on a branch will kill that branch.

Maintenance pruning
This should always be done in late winter or very early spring, some weeks before the buds are due to open. Maintenance pruning in summer will interfere with the tree's system and cause adventitious shoots to emerge where you don't want them. Some pruned areas may collapse and die back.

It's essential to prune the whole tree rather than isolated areas, to

retain the balance of vigour. Prune rather more aggressively toward the top of the tree than on the lower branches. This will further help with the overall balance.

When doing maintenance pruning, remember that you have to allow for the coming season's growth.

The newly pruned tree should look a little thin — as if it had just had a military haircut! Areas that are very dense must be thinned by cutting away congested outer areas so that selected inner shoots can grow to replace them. After several years of careful maintenance pruning, the density of the entire tree will be uniform, and pruning will become an almost mechanical operation — but pleasant, nonetheless.

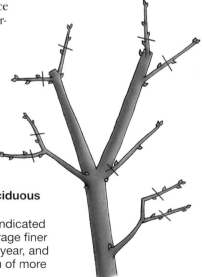

Winter pruning of deciduous trees
Cutting shoots where indicated by red lines will encourage finer and denser twigs next year, and encourages the growth of more adventitious buds.

How to prune

The first rule is always to use clean, sharp tools. Dull, dirty tools will crush the tissues rather than cut them; the wound will not heal well and budding around it will be poor.

Garden secateurs are all right for rough pruning, but they always damage some of the remaining tissue and their design means that a close cut is impossible. Proper bonsai cutters (angled or concave) allow you to cut flush with the remaining wood and even create a slightly hollow wound. Hollow wounds heal flat, so there will be no unsightly lumps of scar tissue on your finished tree.

If you don't have bonsai cutters, arm yourself with a sharp modelling knife for whittling the pruned stub until it is flush with the remaining wood, and slightly hollow. Take special care not to crush or tear the bark around the wound, because this will mean certain die-back.

Sealing the wound

Because the wounds on bonsai should heal perfectly, leaving little or no evidence, fresh wounds should be sealed to keep disease pathogens and frost out, and to keep moisture in.

By far the most effective sealant is Japanese bonsai cut paste. It has the consistency of modelling clay, its colour blends well with the bark, and it contains fungicide to help keep the wound healthy. Cut paste remains soft, so as the wound heals it is gradually pushed off by the callus, or it can be easily removed by hand.

A reasonable substitute can be made by mixing plasticene with a little cooking oil to stop it hardening in the open air. Never on any account use bitumen-based wound paint or any other sealant that dries hard — this will disfigure the tree for years, and any attempt to remove it by hand will cause very noticeable damage to the bark.

Shortening a branch

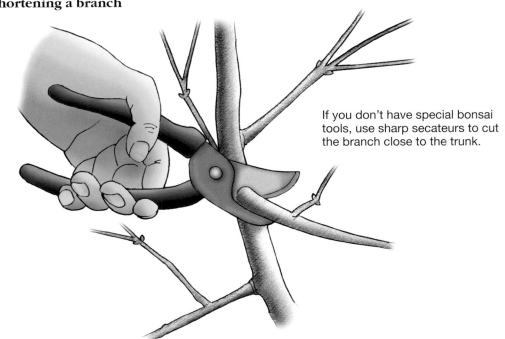

If you don't have special bonsai tools, use sharp secateurs to cut the branch close to the trunk.

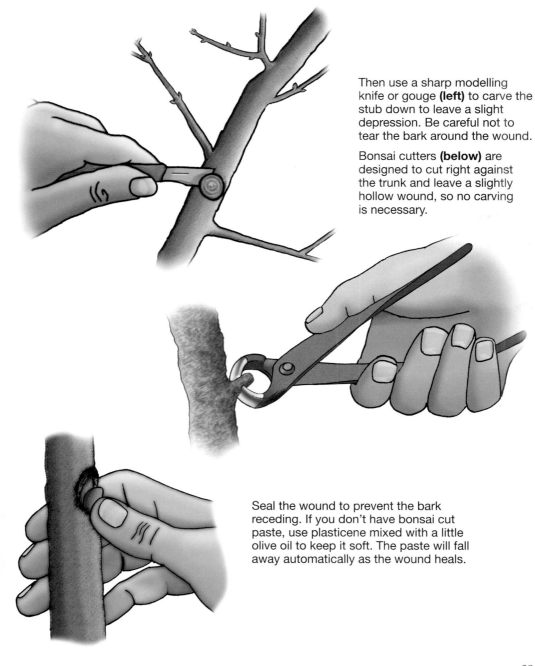

Then use a sharp modelling knife or gouge **(left)** to carve the stub down to leave a slight depression. Be careful not to tear the bark around the wound.

Bonsai cutters **(below)** are designed to cut right against the trunk and leave a slightly hollow wound, so no carving is necessary.

Seal the wound to prevent the bark receding. If you don't have bonsai cut paste, use plasticene mixed with a little olive oil to keep it soft. The paste will fall away automatically as the wound heals.

Pinching shoots

All plants grow, and bonsai are no exception. In the height of summer, as little as a week is long enough for a small bonsai to become over-grown and scruffy.

Bonsai shouldn't just be clipped like a hedge. This will cause over-dense outer foliage and all the valuable inner shoots will die through lack of light. You would then be forced to prune hard and redevelop all the twigs again.

Bonsai must be kept in shape by regular and careful pinching of all the growing tips through-out the growing season. Pinching is the generic term for this operation, although sometimes you will need to resort to sharp shears, while at other times tweezers will make things easier.

In addition to keeping the tree in shape, regular pinching will achieve three further objectives:

1 It allows light and air to reach the inner parts of the tree, enabling the weak inner shoots to grow more strongly, and stimulating dormant and new adventitious buds to grow. This is crucially important in the long term, because you will eventually need to remove larger areas of congested twigs and replace them with the new growth your pinching has stimulated.

2 It prevents the internodes (the length of shoot between leaves) becoming too long. Unless branches are hard-pruned (see page 26), they can only ramify (fork) at an inter-node. Long internodes mean coarse ramifica-tion, which results in a clumpy-looking tree with tufts of foliage at the ends of long branches — not a pleasant sight!

3 Pinching increases ramification. Removing the growing tip of a shoot cuts off the supply of hormones (auxins) produced in the tip.

Auxins suppress the growth of buds further down the shoot and on older wood. In the absence of a flow of auxins, these buds are stimulated to grow.

Deciduous or broadleaved trees

Each time you pinch the tip of a growing shoot on a deciduous tree, two or more smaller, finer shoots will sprout from axils of remaining leaves — and you have two shoots where there was only one. If you pinch twice in the season, then you will have four. At the end of the second year there will be 16, after three years 64, and so on.

Clearly, this process can't continue for ever, otherwise the tree would become so dense that it would probably stifle itself if it didn't take drastic action. This drastic action would consist of shedding branches and throwing out new growth from the base of the trunk.

The increased ramification produced by pinching must be balanced by thinning and rationalisation of the outer areas during main-tenance pruning in late winter (see page 27).

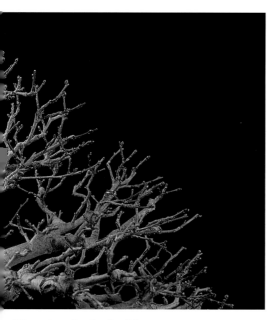

This deciduous tree has already become well ramified thanks to regular pinching, which from now on needs to be carried out more selectively.

If your tree is already well established and has a pleasing shape, you need to be much more disciplined. Watch the buds as they open. The first leaf (or pair of leaves) emerges and at the base of the stem is the tiny bud that contains the next leaf or pair of leaves. The idea is to pluck out this bud as soon as it is big enough to be seen. This is where a pair of tweezers comes in handy.

You don't have to pinch every shoot at one sitting because the buds don't all open at once, but always work over the whole tree every time you pinch. Weak shoots, or those you want to develop further, should be allowed to grow longer and should retain more leaves after pinching.

How to pinch deciduous or broadleaved trees

If you're still developing branches, wait until the shoots have three or four internodes and then pinch back to the first internode on opposite-leaved trees such as maples, or to the second internode on alternate-leaved trees, such as elms.

Conifers

Conifers react rather differently from broadleaved trees, even though the result is the same. They don't have buds at every leaf axil — there are so many needles or scales clothing the shoots that it would be ridiculous. Some lateral

Pinching new growth

Broadleaved trees
Pinch out the tiny bud at the tip of the shoot as soon as the first pair of leaves has hardened. You may need to use tweezers for this.

buds do exist on the shoots, but they are in predetermined locations. Moreover, each conifer species reacts in its own individual way to pinching.

Pines

Pines are unique insofar as they rarely have pre-existing lateral buds on shoots. They are also unique in that they are genetically programmed to have only one flush of growth a year. These two factors share a common cause. Pines are late to begin growth, their shoots take longer to mature, and their buds take a lot longer to become ready to sprout.

When you pinch a pine shoot — or *candle* as it is known — buds form around the point where the shoot is severed. This is great news, because it means you can shorten a shoot to precisely where you want it to fork. New buds will also appear on the previous year's growth and, if you're lucky and the tree is healthy, on even older wood.

How to pinch pines

Pine buds don't open in quite the same way as those on other trees. They extend into candles, with the tiny embryonic needles pressed flat to the stem, held in place by a papery sheath. As the candles continue to lengthen, they slowly mature, and the needles begin to pull away from the central shoot. Now is the time to start thinking about pinching.

If you need to induce buds on older growth, you should allow the candles to extend and the needles to peel away until they are standing at an angle of about 45 degrees from the shoot. Then cut the entire shoot off, leaving just a half dozen or so needles at the base (you will need sharp shears for this). New buds will form on older growth during the autumn and winter, ready for next spring.

If you want to develop ramification, wait until the needles are just beginning to peel away and are standing at about 15 degrees from the shoot. Then pinch back to the point where you want the shoot to fork. New buds will form at the severed end of the shoot.

If your bonsai pine is already established and you want to retain and refine its form, you should attack earlier. The ideal time is just as the papery sheath begins to fall away — the shoots will still be short and soft, and the needles will only just be discernible. Then new buds will form at the severed end of the shoot and around its base. Some will also appear on older wood.

Pinching new growth

Pines
Wait until the developing 'candles' are long enough to handle, and break them by bending and twisting at the same time.

Pinching new growth

Junipers

Juniper foliage is very fine and dense. Hold a 'fan' of shoots between the thumb and forefinger of one hand, and pull away the tips with the other.

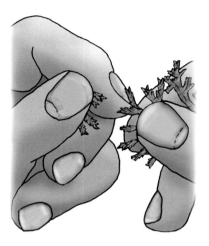

Junipers

Junipers can have either needle or scale foliage, but whichever is the case, about one-third of the leaves will have tiny buds in their axils.

New shoot generation is usually prolific. Junipers continue growing steadily from spring until well into autumn. If you keep a juniper in a *cool* greenhouse or conservatory during winter, it will grow all year round.

How to pinch junipers

Pinching junipers is really easy in one respect. They have such short internodes that the pre-existing buds, although few in number compared to the number of leaves, are very close together and itching to sprout.

In another respect junipers are hard work, because they are continuously growing and pinching becomes a weekly routine.

The technique, though, is simple. Just grasp a fan of shoots between thumb and finger with one hand, and pull off the tips with the other. Every so often you'll need to use the point of your shears to cut out the plump, vigorous shoots from the centres of the foliage clusters, so that the younger, fresher shoots have space to grow.

Flat-needle conifers

Yew, hemlock, larch, some cedars

Like junipers, most flat-needle conifers have buds at about one-third of the leaf axils. Many, though, are capable of generating adventitious buds on older growth as well in axils that didn't originally have buds. At one end of the scale, larch almost never bud on old wood, whereas yew do this so prolifically that it can become a real nuisance.

How to pinch flat-needle conifers

On developing trees, allow shoots to grow until they are almost as dark in colour as the old foliage, then cut back to roughly the point where you want a fork. There are bound to be some viable buds in the near vicinity of the severance point, even if you can't see them.

On established trees, pinch back hard when the shoots are about 25–30 mm long. Leave three or four needles — no more. Within a few weeks, a new crop of finer, neater shoots will sprout from all over the place.

Sharp-needle conifers

Spruce, some cedars

Species in this category have some pre-formed buds in leaf axils, but fewer than with flat-needle species. What buds do exist are widely spaced and sprout at right angles to the parent shoot, making for a very untidy foliage mass. These trees need to be approached in a special way, using a cycle of removal and re-growth.

If you shorten a shoot to below the first lateral bud, so there are no more buds remaining on that shoot (which you will have to do to keep the tree in trim), no new buds will form and the shoot will abort during the following year. This isn't so much of a problem as it might sound.

New buds will form at the base of the shoot and on older wood. The following spring, the aborted shoots are cut out completely and a new crop of shorter shoots emerges. These may be so short that they don't need pinching. When the buds at the tips of these shoots sprout during the third spring, then the cycle will be repeated.

How to pinch sharp-needle conifers
Since the pinched shoots will abort next year, there's nothing to be gained by leaving them so long that the tree looks untidy, regardless of whether your tree is established or still in the ramification process. The difference is in the timing.

To increase ramification, allow the shoot to mature, then remove it completely. Masses of new buds will form at the shoot base and on old wood.

To refine and maintain, pinch out the shoots as soon as they are large enough to handle with tweezers. Leave just a rosette of needles about three layers thick — say, no more than a dozen. As you work over the tree, cut out all last year's pinched shoots, which by now will be looking a little sad. Healthy trees may push out a second flush of growth later in the summer. These shoots will be beautifully small and fine, and will probably not need pinching.

Pinching new growth

Spruce
The shoots emerge like tiny green shaving brushes. As soon as they are big enough to handle, pull out the tips by hand, leaving about a third behind.

Spruce bonsai need to be pinched in a special way, following a three-year cycle.

Repotting

This is the one aspect of bonsai that scares off the novice and provokes the 'bonsai is cruel' brigade. But it is an absolutely essential operation — not to stunt the tree's growth, but to keep it in perfect health and growing strongly.

All trees need to be able to extend their roots annually. If a bonsai is overdue for repotting, the pot itself will be jam-packed with roots. With no room to extend, and the poor drainage and aeration that pot-bound roots create, the root system will deteriorate. Decay will set in, living roots will begin to rot, the soil will become sour and full of pathogens, and the tree will eventually die.

The frequency of repotting and, to a certain extent, the timing, depends on the age, size and species of each tree. Young or small bonsai need to be repotted annually — especially tropical or subtropical species that grow more or less all year round. Larger trees and older trees may only need repotting every two or three years. Really old bonsai may only need repotting once every four years or so.

When to repot

Gardeners will tell you that autumn is the time to bare-root and replant trees. But if you cut the roots in autumn, the tree has to wait three or four months before the roots can regenerate. All the wounds will be left open to infection, frost damage and decay. The traditional gardening practice of autumn transplanting probably has more to do with the lack of other things to do at that time of year.

The only sure way to tell if your tree needs repotting is to inspect the roots (see page 39), but first here are some rough guidelines to start off with:

Hardy deciduous species

These should be repotted every one or two years, depending on the age and size or your tree. Repot in late winter or very early spring — ideally before the buds begin to swell. You can repot after the buds start swelling, but as soon as they begin to show green, root-pruning will interrupt growth and some shoots may be lost.

Pines

Pine roots grow quite slowly, so even small pine bonsai can live happily in the same soil for two or three years before repotting is necessary. Larger or older pines should only be repotted every four or five years. Too-frequent repotting will retard the growth of most pines.

You should repot in mid to late spring, before or just as the buds show the first signs of elongating into candles.

Junipers

Once established in a bonsai pot, junipers are happy to remain in the same soil for years. However, they will gradually deteriorate — slowly and almost indiscernibly. Don't be fooled. Maintain health by repotting small trees every two years and larger trees every three or four years.

Mid to late spring is the best time for repotting, although junipers can be repotted fairly safely in early summer.

Other hardy conifers

Spruce, yew, hemlock etc. should be repotted every two years if they are small to medium-sized, and every three to four if they are larger or very old. Repot in late winter or early spring.

Subtropicals and tropicals

Small to medium-size trees need repotting annually, and others every two years. Much depends on growth rate, which can vary tremendously according to the conditions in your home or conservatory. Generally speaking, spring is the best time, because the increased light levels tend to increase the growth rate. However, if conditions are fairly consistent all year round, subtropical and tropical species can be repotted at more or less any time.

Preparation

Before you start, make sure you have everything you'll need to finish the job. There's nothing worse for the tree than being left with its roots exposed to the air while you drive around local nurseries and garden centres looking for that elusive thing that you thought you had but didn't. You will need the following:

• a root hook, chopsticks, knitting needles or similar device for teasing out the roots and old soil

• sharp root shears for cutting roots (don't use your twig shears or branch cutters on roots, because the grit in the soil will blunt them in next to no time)

• a bowl of water to dunk the roots in to wash away the old loose soil and to keep the roots moist while you work (a spray bottle is also useful for this)

• a new pot — or else the same pot thoroughly cleaned (see page 42)

• rigid mesh to cover the drainage holes

• some wire to hold the mesh in place

• natural-fibre string to tie the tree into the pot

• an adequate supply of fresh soil (see opposite)

• a watering can with a fine-rose sprinkler.

Bonsai pots

A bonsai pot is more than just a container for the tree. It's an integral part of the composition and must be aesthetically harmonious with the design of the tree, as well as being horticulturally adequate.

Bonsai pots come in a wide range of shapes, sizes and colours, each with its own advantages and disadvantages. The picture below shows the some of the wide variety of pot designs that are available on the market.

All bonsai pots must have good drainage — much larger holes than you would expect to see in a normal flower pot. Pots that are for hardy trees should also be frost-proof — i.e. they should be of stoneware rather than earthenware. Water soaks into earthenware and shatters it when it freezes in winter.

As far as colour is concerned, that is more a matter of personal taste. Having said that, it's always best to choose subdued, earthy colours that won't be too overpowering and dominate the tree.

Bonsai soil

Different species are said to have slightly different soil requirements, but all will grow well in a standard bonsai soil. Only when you are hooked on bonsai will you need to tinker with the recipe. Pines, for example, like a more sandy soil. Junipers appreciate a little more humus (organic matter). Flowering species prefer a slightly denser growing medium. But all will do perfectly well in a standard soil.

Akadama

Nowadays, most specialist nurseries and garden centres that deal with bonsai paraphernalia will sell an imported Japanese soil called *akadama*.

*Bonsai pots (**left**) are sold in a wide variety of shapes, sizes and colours. Among the commonest shapes are hexagonal, oval and rectangular. They also include the much smaller* mame *pots and the taller varieties suitable for cascade-style bonsai.*

*Akadama from Japan is by far the best soil for bonsai, but it can often be very expensive, so you may well prefer to mix your own soil (**below**).*

This is a granular, clay-like volcanic substance that retains its particle structure even when wet.

Akadama can be expensive, but it is very good indeed. Some enthusiasts use it for all their trees, others never use it, and some use it as an ingredient in a more general mix. Although akadama is a near-perfect soil for bonsai, it is far cheaper and more or less as effective to mix your own soil.

Mixing your own soil
Before you begin, it's important to understand the requirements for bonsai soil.

First, it must be coarse: particles between 2 mm and 4 mm in diameter are ideal. This allows for two of the essential requirements: rapid drainage and ample air spaces.

Second, the particles themselves must be able to absorb water and nutrients, and release them to the roots as they are needed.

Third, it must be horticulturally clean. This doesn't mean that the ingredients must be inert, but that they must be free of pathogens and impurities.

The basic soil mix for bonsai used to consist of equal parts of sifted peat and grit. Nowadays, however, we are aware that peat extraction is environmentally hostile, and everyone who cares about that sort of thing, as most bonsai lovers do, has sought alternatives to peat. This has resulted in an even better standard of mix that is both environmentally friendly and suitable for a much broader range of species and growing conditions.

 Important

Always dry the soil ingredients before sifting and mixing them. This will ensure that no dust remains adhered to the larger particles, and besides it is much easier to work with dry soil than wet, sticky muck!

Bonsai soil mix

The basic ingredients for bonsai soil are as follows:

- 40% horticultural grit
- 40% crushed bark
- 20% calcined clay soil conditioner.

40% horticultural grit
Don't use crushed granite, because this decomposes chemically and releases some mild toxins. Flint grit is best. An alternative is coarse sand that has been well sifted and washed.

40% crushed bark
The type used by orchid growers is perfect. Ask for the smallest grade. Any over-size particles can easily be rubbed through a sieve. If you can't find orchid bark easily, you can use pine-needle mould or oak-leaf mould, but you will find there is a lot of wastage when you sift it.

20% calcined clay soil conditioner
This ingredient is much easier to find than you might imagine. Calcined clay is simply ordinary clay that has been baked so that it retains its granular structure but still absorbs vast amounts of water.

Most garden centres will stock one brand or another, but if you have problems finding a stockist, try the pet shop!

Cat litter of the kind known as fuller's earth is a form of calcined clay. While not quite as good as the horticultural variety, it will certainly do the job. But it's best make sure you buy the unperfumed, non-clumping kind. The last thing you want is for your bonsai soil to congeal into a gooey lump as soon as it is watered — regardless of how sweet it might smell!

Getting stuck in

Inspecting the roots

There's no point in repotting for the sake of it, but neither should you let your bonsai go too long without repotting. Your decision will depend on the state of the roots.

The only way to see how dense the roots are is by looking at them. Grasp the base of the trunk and see if you can very gently pull the tree from the pot. Tilting the trunk slightly might help, but if it feels at all reluctant to budge, don't tug too hard — push a flat blade between the pot and the soil and work it all around the root mass. With a round or oval pot, you'll need to use a thinner blade.

If you see a solid mass of roots coiled around the soil, repotting is definitely in order. If the root mass looks like a coconut doormat, it's also time to repot. If there are some healthy-looking roots but you can still see plenty of soil particles, then repotting can wait another year.

 Important

If on inspection you see very few roots and the soil falls away in lumps, then something is wrong. Any tree that has been in a bonsai pot for a year or more should have much more root — certainly enough to hold the soil in one cohesive mass. If your bonsai is in this condition, you should repot immediately without disturbing the existing roots any more than you can help. Then re-assess your watering and feeding schedule, and check the drainage of the pot. Something is causing the roots to decay, so you need to find out what and rectify it.

Inspecting the roots

Hold the tree by the base of the trunk and gently ease it from the pot. If the roots appear dense and tight, then it is due for repotting.

Never repot bonsai until you've inspected the roots. In this case the tree is definitely rootbound and in need of repotting.

Removing the old soil

Rule number one is be gentle! Some people stab away frantically at the roots with sharp hooks as if they were competing in a race. Sometimes dense roots can be a bit tiresome, but the more care you take the better.

Start at the bottom edge, untangling the coiled roots all around the root mass. These will be cut off eventually, so if some break now it doesn't really matter. Once these long roots have been pulled away, the soil around the bottom edge will be easier to comb out.

Work your way up the side of the root mass, removing soil uniformly all around it. When you get to the top edge, begin working your way toward the trunk. Comb the roots outward as

you work — and be patient! At all costs avoid tearing at the tougher surface roots.

Finally you should attend to the underside. Remove proportionally as much soil here as you did at the sides. In fact, the higher you can get in the centre, the better. This is the last area to become colonised by new root growth and good fresh soil is more inviting.

By the time you have finished, you should have removed about a half to two-thirds of the total volume of soil.

If the soil is heavy or that slimy grey Chinese clay, then you'd be well advised to remove all of it. The job is time-consuming but well worth it in the long term — it's far easier to control

Removing the old soil

Use a chopstick, root hook or similar tool to comb the old soil from the roots. Work all around the root mass and pay special attention to the underside. Remove about two-thirds of the soil volume.

watering and feeding in a soil that is uniform throughout the pot. The best way of removing old dense bonsai soil is by dunking the roots in water to saturate the soil and then playing a fine, strong jet of water on it. Larger trees can he hosed in the garden, but the smaller, more delicate ones are best attended to with a spray bottle, keeping the nozzle fully open.

Cutting the roots

This is the really delicate part of the job. The principle is to trim the long, straggly roots so the tree will fit back in the pot with enough space around the root mass to accommodate a good supply of fresh soil. With small bonsai, 15 mm or so should do; larger trees should have more space.

That's the basic principle, but it isn't always quite so straightforward. If you just trimmed all the roots equally, like clipping a hedge, after a few years you would have a pot full of thick, clumpy roots with little tufts of fine feeding roots at the ends. The idea is to encourage the feeding roots to colonise the entire pot for maximum efficiency, so you need to be a little more subtle in your approach.

Cut thick roots first, and cut them further back. Many of the fine roots will be growing on lateral roots, which in turn merge from the thick roots closer to the trunk. Cut the thick roots back to where these laterals emerge, leaving the laterals intact.

Use your discretion — in total, you should remove between one-third and a half of the original rootage. If cutting the thick roots back hard looks as if it's going to eliminate more than half the fine roots, leave some thick roots longer and shorten them next time round. By reducing the thick roots systematically, you will encourage the generation of more fine roots, closer to the trunk. This is an ongoing process, because today's thin roots will be tomorrow's thick roots.

Once you have attended to the thick roots, you can trim the finer roots. These can be cut like a fringe, but make sure your shears are sharp, because some roots (on elms in particular) are stringy and can easily become mashed by blunt blades.

Finally, spray the roots or dunk them in water to keep them moist while you prepare the pot.

Cutting the finer roots

Use sharp scissors to cut back all the long straggly roots until the remaining mass fits easily in the pot with an inch or so gap all around.

Preparing the pot

The pot must first be thoroughly cleaned, including underneath, where all manner of bugs can lurk.

Then you need to fix some mesh over the drainage holes to prevent the soil from washing out. Most bonsai dealers will sell plastic mesh for this purpose, but any fairly rigid mesh with about 3-mm holes will do just fine. Cut the mesh to about 12 mm wider than the drainage hole all round.

Then take a piece of thin wire, and fashion it into a staple with loops at the corners. Push the staple through the mesh, down through the drainage hole and bend it over to secure the mesh firmly.

Traditionally, wire is pushed up through the drainage holes (or through the small wire holes that some pots have) for use later to tie the tree into the pot. I personally prefer to use natural-fibre string. With time, wire can cut into the

Preparing the pot

Clean the pot thoroughly and cover the drainage holes with mesh. Then insert tying wires (or string) through the drainage holes.

roots, especially if the repotting schedule is every three or four years. String will decay by the end of the first summer, so the roots are free of danger. By the time the string has decayed, the new roots will have grown enough to hold the tree firmly in the pot.

Drape the string or wire over the edges of the pot, and add a layer of soil in the bottom. Make a small mound of soil just off the centre of the pot. This should be the point directly beneath where the trunk will sit.

Now you're ready to replant the tree.

 Adding soil

There's no need to worry about a drainage course of larger particles. This is an old gardening practice that has long been discredited. Your coarse soil will provide all the drainage you need for bonsai.

Replanting 1

Place a layer of soil in the base of the pot, mounding it slightly just off centre. Then position the tree and nestle it down into the soil by twisting it a few times.

Replanting 2

Add some more soil and tighten the tying wires over the roots to hold the tree firm (wires can be cut off in a couple of months).

Replanting the tree

Drain any excess water from the roots before replanting. Pick up the tree by pushing your fingers under the root mass, spreading the roots outward as you do so, then lift. The purpose of lifting the tree this way is to ensure that there are no 'ingrowing' roots tucked underneath.

Set the tree down on the mound of soil in the pot. Now gently twist and rock the tree, holding it at the base of the trunk. This settles the tree into the soil and works soil particles into the spaces beneath the trunk.

Pay attention to the planting angle. Make sure the tree is facing front and that the trunk doesn't lean more than it should. When you're satisfied with the planting angle, and that the tree is settled to the right depth in the pot, bring the string (or wire) over the roots and tie them securely — but not so tight as to crush the roots. If possible, work the string between thick roots and secure the tree as close to the trunk as you can.

Replacing the soil

This is where you'll need your chopstick again. Add soil around and over the roots a handful at a time. As you add the soil, work it in between the roots with the chopstick. Insert the chopstick through the soil and between roots, and move

it in a circular motion. Whatever you do, don't stab at the roots or you will cause unnecessary damage. Continue adding soil and working it among the roots until the pot is full to just below the rim and you're confident there are no empty spaces within the core of the roots. Now you're almost done.

After-care

You now need to water your bonsai thoroughly but gently. The soil particles will wash away easily at this stage because there are no roots holding them together, so be careful. Water slowly with a spray or a fine rose on a watering can. Saturate the soil, wait

for ten minutes and repeat; then repeat once more. This ensures that all the dry soil particles are thoroughly soaked.

From now on, keep the tree away from frost. If you keep the tree indoors, avoid heat and direct sun until it has started growing again.

Don't feed newly repotted trees for about six weeks, or at least until the tree has established new growth. The presence of fertiliser in the soil actually retards root generation. If the tree was sickly when you repotted, you can apply some foliar feed after a week or so — though this wouldn't of course apply to deciduous species.

Replacing the soil

Work the fresh soil in between all the roots with a chopstick. Be careful not to stab the roots as you do so.

Basic wiring

Why wire?

Wiring is the primary technique used to shape the young trunks, branches and shoots of bonsai. The principle is straightforward. Wire is coiled around the trunk or branch to be shaped. The branch and wire are then bent into shape, and the wire holds the branch in position. The new wood that is deposited as the tree grows will, in theory, hold the branch in position once the wire is removed — in theory because some species take longer to 'set' than others.

How long does it take?

The time necessary for wire training to have a permanent effect on branch shape depends on the species, the age and vigour of the tree, and the thickness of the branch — so there is no short answer to this question. But here are a few broad generalisations:

- Conifers take a lot longer to set than broadleaved trees. This has something to do with the fact that the greater resin content makes the branches springier (which is why conifers are used for making longbows).

- Slow-growing trees of whatever type will take longer to set than faster-growing trees of the same type.

- The thicker the branch, the longer it will take to set.

- The older the branch, the longer it will take to set.

Taking two extremes, a young green shoot on a vigorous Chinese elm or Japanese maple wired in early summer will set in position within three weeks or so — whereas a ten-year-old juniper branch will probably take six to ten years and require annual rewiring.

Applying the wire

Whatever wire you choose to use (see page 24), the application method is the same.

Choosing the right thickness

With experience, you will soon be able to tell just by looking at a branch what gauge of wire it will need. But to begin with, rather than adopt the trial-and-error approach, there is a simple test you can apply. Try

Wiring a complex set of branches like these is not always easy but is invariably rewarding, and as with everything practice makes perfect.

Practice makes perfect

Before you embark on your first foray into the delights of wire-shaping trees — it is indeed a very rewarding, if laborious operation — you would be wise to practise first on some twigs from one of your garden shrubs.

Try to choose something that has similar-sized shoots and branches to the tree you intend to work on. Cut something big enough so you can tie the thick end to a chair or something, to make it stable to work on.

Try several different thicknesses of wire. Practise judging what gauge to use. Wire the whole twig, thick and thin, following the instructions shown in the step-by-step illustrations overleaf, then remove the wire and do it again. This may sound a little draconian, but this practice period really is important.

Once you feel you have the hang of it — your wiring is neat and your fingers are limbered up — then it's time to take the plunge.

testing the resistance of the branch or shoot with your fingers, then try testing some wire with the same fingers. If the two seem similar, or even if the wire seems at first to be a little easier to bend, then you have the right gauge. If the wire bends much more easily, then it's clearly too thin. If it feels at all stiffer than the branch, it's too thick.

Perhaps the obvious question is 'What if I don't have the correct gauge?' Well, you can either use a thicker wire or use two strands of a thinner one. But always remember that the strength of the two alternatives isn't the same: two strands of 2-mm wire will only have 60% of the holding strength of one strand of 4-mm wire. Moreover, using more than two strands of wire is highly undesirable, both for aesthetic reasons and because it risks strangling the branch.

Some tricks of the trade

The illustrations show you how to apply the wire and work out which wire goes where. But there are a few tips and pointers that will help make your wiring easier and more effective:

• The length of wire you'll need for any given branch is about one-and-a-half times the length of the branch. This allows you a little extra at the tip to make handling easier.

• Coil the wire at about a 45-degree angle for maximum holding and economy.

• Start with the thickest wire, and apply it wherever it is needed all over the tree, before moving on to the second-thickest.

• When using two parallel strands of wire, apply them one at a time — and leave no space between them.

• When you are using one wire for two branches, make sure the branches are far enough apart for the wire to spiral around the trunk (or parent branch) at least one-and-a-half full turns.

• When wiring the fine shoots, always end the wire in a small loop around the shoot. This will stop the shoot from springing out of the wire coil.

• Finally, wiring doesn't have to be perfect in order to do the job perfectly, but it does help.

Wiring — right and wrong

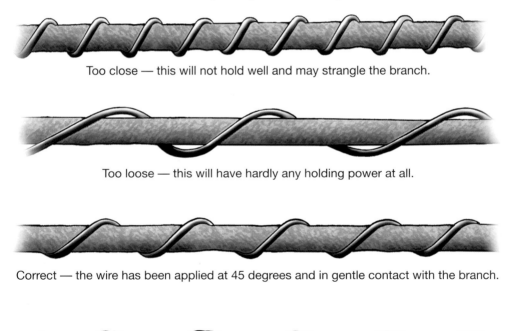

Too close — this will not hold well and may strangle the branch.

Too loose — this will have hardly any holding power at all.

Correct — the wire has been applied at 45 degrees and in gentle contact with the branch.

If one wire won't hold, another can be applied directly alongside the first.

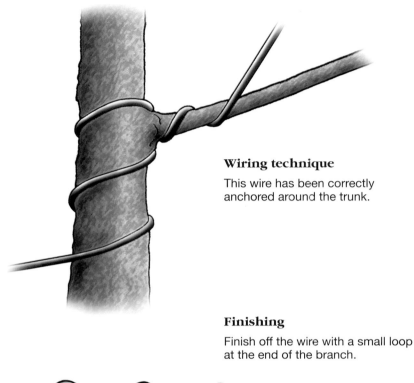

Wiring technique

This wire has been correctly
anchored around the trunk.

Finishing

Finish off the wire with a small loop
at the end of the branch.

When to remove the wire

Judging when to remove the wire requires fairly
close observation. It's not a case of leaving it
until the branch has set in position, because
you need to remove the wire *before* it has
begun to dig into the bark as the branch swells.

The wire will begin to cut into the bark first
on the more vigorous branches, usually at the
top of the tree. As soon as you notice these
wires looking tighter than those on the lower or
weaker branches, you should start removing

them. If they haven't marked the bark, then you
know you can leave the wire on the lower
branches for longer. If, on the other hand, the
branches that are free of wire spring back into
their original positions (this may take an hour
or two, so 'spring' is hardly the right word),
then you should re-wire them, preferably
coiling the wire in the opposite direction in
order to avoid following the same pressure
lines as before.

The scarring on this tree shows that the wire was left on too long. Always make sure you remove it before it starts to dig into the branches.

Removing the wire

Always *cut* the wire off the tree once it's done its job. *Never* try to unwind it — except during practice sessions. Unwinding the wire is very likely to snap branches, strip bark and dislodge buds. Your bonsai is worth more than a few inches of salvaged wire.

Advanced wiring

Ordinary wiring techniques aren't always sufficient for what you need to do. Sometimes you may want to reposition major branches, or perhaps just introduce a bend in a heavy branch to relieve the line. Thick branches can require special treatment to get them to bend and hold their position.

When deciding which technique to employ, you need to consider the species. Non-conifers are generally more brittle than conifers. Whereas conifers will show small splits in the bark before they break, most non-conifers are less obliging. They bend and then they break with little or no warning.

Bending thick non-coniferous branches requires much more time, increasing the bend every so often until you achieve the desired shape. Clamps or ties (see pages 54-5) are the best technique for this.

Thick conifer branches can usually be manipulated into their final positions in one session using the raffia technique.

The raffia technique

This technique was developed for use on wild conifers whose foliage was limited to the tips of long branches. To compact the tree into an acceptable bonsai format, extreme bending was

The raffia technique is a rather more drastic method of wiring that is generally only suitable for use with conifers.

needed. Some non-conifers can also be treated this way, but it's generally best to gain some experience before attempting that.

The raffia (strips of inner bark from the raphia palm) is first soaked to soften it, and is then bound tightly around the branch to be bent. Laying some longitudinal strands of raffia along the branch on the outside of the intended bend, beneath the binding, will increase its effectiveness. Heavy wire is then coiled around the branch in the normal way.

The raffia holds the bark tight to the sapwood, preventing it from slipping as the branch is bent. The tension provided by

the longitudinal strands helps to stop the bark on the outside of the bend from stretching to splitting point.

This technique is by no means foolproof, and considerable care is needed to execute it successfully. So before attempting it on anything valuable, you should first experiment on an unwanted branch on a plant of the same species.

Branch splitting

This technique enables you to alter the angle of elevation of a branch immediately against the trunk. Branches that leave the trunk at an upward angle and arch over to point down don't look good, and will spoil the

Branch splitting may seem a rather drastic technique for changing the angle of a branch, but it works well if carried out with care.

tree. Branches that slope downward look better if they do so right from the start.

The sap flow into and out of a branch takes place from below. There is little or no sap flow from the branch to or from the trunk above. This means that, in theory, you could dispense with the purely structural connection on the upper side of the branch. The theory actually works in practice, but you need to be very brave — and very careful.

In spring, take a very fine saw — a hacksaw blade would be good — and cut a slot in the top of the 'collar' where branch meets trunk. Slant the cut inward at about 30 degrees from vertical.

Hold the trunk with your thumb pressed firmly against it immediately below the branch. Now pull the branch down until you see the cut begin to open, watch carefully for signs of the cut splitting too much further and then stop pulling.

Wedge a small stone or piece of wire into the widened slot to hold it open, and wire the branch to the trunk for safety. After two months' growth, you can pull the branch down a little further, and again the following spring, and so on. Keep the wound well plugged with cut paste to keep water out. Eventually it will heal completely with the stone or wire still inside.

Mitre cuts

This technique is even more delicate than branch splitting. But if you need to make a sharp bend at a point where clamps won't do the job, this is the method to use. It can be used to make hairpin bends in more supple species like pine and larch, but you should

never try it with junipers because it simply won't work.

As soon as the tree has settled into growth in spring, cut a wedge from the inside of the anticipated bend with a fine saw. The wedge has to be at least half-way through the branch — but don't overdo it!

You need to judge the width of the wedge carefully: it must be tightly closed once the branch is bent. If you make it too wide, the branch won't set

in position and may well die. If you make it too narrow, the branch won't bend far enough or the bark will split on the other side.

Once you've bent the branch, hold it in position with wire or ties — whichever is appropriate. But the cut must always be tightly closed. To reward you for your care and diligence, the wound will heal and the branch will be set in position by winter.

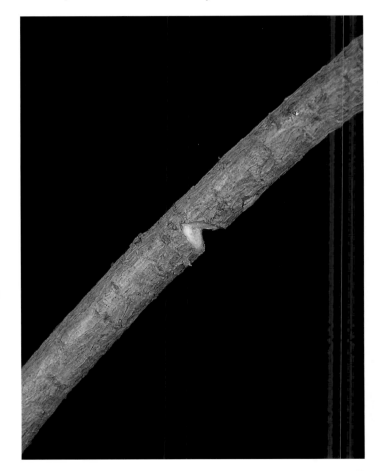

A mitre cut involves sawing a small wedge out of a branch to create a sharp bend, and it should only be tried with the supplest of trees.

Other bending techniques

Branch clamps

These ingenious clamps are custom-designed for bending bonsai branches. They operate on a very simple principle and introduce an angular bend rather than a smooth curve. They can be used on any tree species but are especially useful for bending non-coniferous branches, the main advantage being that you can increase the bend periodically simply by turning one of the wing nuts. The branches set in position quite quickly when

Above *Branch clamps are specially designed for bending bonsai branches.*

Left *Ties and tourniquets are the gentlest method but also the least accurate.*

clamps are used, because all the bending takes place at one point and the maximum emergency tissue is deposited around the bend.

Although the two hooks and the push plate are padded with plastic, they still create considerable pressure on the bark. So you should always use additional padding to protect the bark, such as small patches cut from old rubber boots.

Most bonsai retailers stock branch clamps, or will be able to get them for you.

Ties and tourniquets

This is the gentlest method of bending branches, but also the slowest and most imprecise. Ties and tourniquets are gentle because they simply pull the entire branch into position, allowing it to bend where it wants to. They are imprecise

wood — but as the whole contraption looks a little bizarre, that probably won't matter. You'll also need some small spacers — wooden blocks, pieces of Lego, anything will do — and of course plenty of padding.

One advantage of this technique is that you can adapt it to suit the circumstances. You can either use one spacer between the bar and the trunk, at the point of the bend (see illustration), or you can use a spacer at each end of the bar. Whichever method you choose, the result will be the same. An additional bonus is that you can adjust the tension periodically, in the same way as with clamps. But whatever you do, be sure to use plenty of padding.

because they need to be anchored somewhere else on the tree — a heavy root or branch, for example — and some compromise over position is inevitable. They are slow because there are no stress points where large amounts of emergency tissue are deposited.

You can use either one wire or two — or fine nylon thread for better appearance. When two wires are used, they can be twisted together to increase the tension periodically. Make sure you use plenty of padding to cushion the bark from the considerable pressure that a tight tourniquet can exert.

Block and tackle

This rather Heath Robinson method is a good substitute for clamps when none are available, or where clamps can't be used for reasons of lack of space. It is best used for really heavy branches or trunks.

You will need a rigid bar of wood or metal. Metal is better because it doesn't need to be so thick and cumbersome as

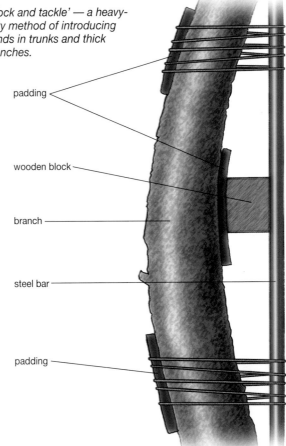

'Block and tackle' — a heavy-duty method of introducing bends in trunks and thick branches.

padding

wooden block

branch

steel bar

padding

Shaping by pruning

Wiring is not the only way to shape branches. In China, the Lignan school of bonsai employs pruning alone. Pruning is a much slower method of shaping branches than wiring, but arguably produces the most satisfactory result in the long term.

Shoots are allowed to grow until they become woody and then cut hard back to a bud that is facing in the direction that you want the new section of branch to grow. Obviously, the chances of having a bud facing in the right direction in the right place are pretty slim, so

you will usually have to compromise by cutting back further, to the next-best bud, and then re-growing that section again. This is what makes the process slow.

After sufficient time, and with sufficient patience, you will develop a branch formation that is wonderfully gnarled, angular and full of beautiful shapes. It will be far more natural and infinitely more interesting that any wire-trained branch formation could ever be.

Predicting future growth
Initial branches are developed by being allowed to grow for several years before you cut back and select some of the randomly regenerated shoots for further training. This is where growth

Predicting future growth

When a branch is pruned to leave a short stub, the dormant buds at its base will soon sprout new shoots.

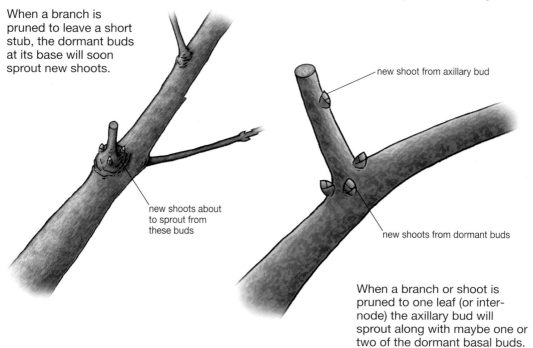

new shoots about to sprout from these buds

new shoot from axillary bud

new shoots from dormant buds

When a branch or shoot is pruned to one leaf (or inter-node) the axillary bud will sprout along with maybe one or two of the dormant basal buds.

prediction comes in. Trees are usually highly predictable in their response to considered pruning. Buds will always grow in the direction they're facing, so you can predict with accuracy which direction the new shoot will take. When you prune a shoot or a one-year-old twig back to a visible bud, then that bud will always sprout another shoot. Other buds further back on the pruned twig may also sprout, but you can rely absolutely on the one at the tip.

If there is no convenient bud, you can cut the twig back to its base, leaving a short stub. Around the base of the stub you'll see some ridges in the bark where the original bud scales fell. Here there will be many dormant buds, but the two strongest — therefore the first to grow — will be at either side of the stub, rather than in the angle between the twig and the parent branch. So you know that if you rub off one of these buds as soon as you see it — if it's not already visible — the other will grow strongly.

The more you cut back hard and re-grow, the more gnarled and interesting your branch shapes will be.

Timing

You can also predict how strong new growth will be by the timing of your pruning.

Pruning tender young shoots is tantamount to pinching, and results in finer, less vigorous growth.

Pruning just as the shoot begins to change colour at its base — around midsummer — will induce more vigorous growth that will itself become woody by the end of the summer. In many species, this can be pruned again to generate yet another set of new shoots which should be able to harden of before the autumn.

Tropicals and subtropicals kept indoors can be expected to respond to pruning all year round, although their response in winter will be slower.

Pruning to buds on hardy species in winter will generate very strong growth from the terminal buds, and some slightly weaker growth from other buds on or near the pruned twigs.

This 30-year-old English elm has been shaped by the author to conform with the classical broom style, which is based on the natural shape of the zelkova (see page 61).

Classic styles

Although the main purpose of making your own bonsai is to create a tree that is pleasing to you, you may want to follow one of the classic Japanese styles. It is certainly worth learning them, because they were developed over many years and following their 'rules' usually leads to a good result. Only when you know the rules can you break them.

There are five main classic bonsai styles, all based on trunk configuration. In addition to these, there are neo-classic styles, such as forest style and broom style, which should also be included.

Formal upright

The trunk is bolt upright and gently tapered from the base to the apex. Branches are arranged evenly all around the trunk, leaving the front clear of branches below the halfway point.

Informal upright

The trunk is gently tapered from the base to the apex, and includes a series of 'S' curves which diminish toward the top of the tree. Branches are arranged evenly all around the trunk, leaving the front clear of branches below the halfway point.

Classic styles 1

Formal upright style

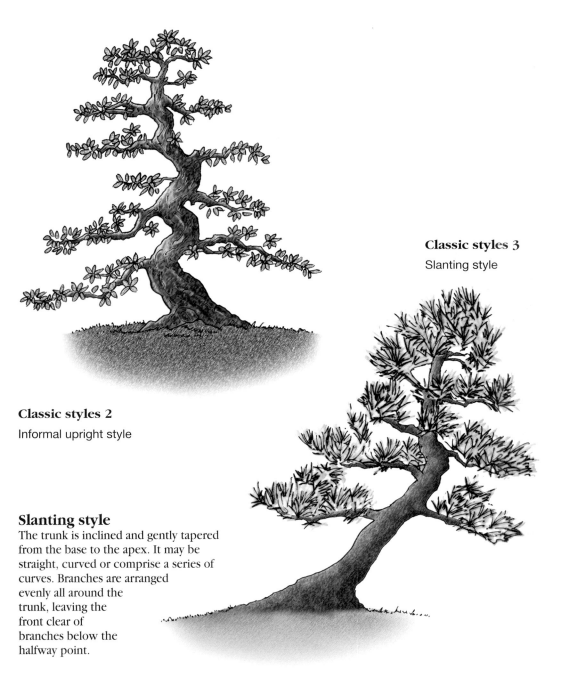

Classic styles 3

Slanting style

Classic styles 2

Informal upright style

Slanting style

The trunk is inclined and gently tapered from the base to the apex. It may be straight, curved or comprise a series of curves. Branches are arranged evenly all around the trunk, leaving the front clear of branches below the halfway point.

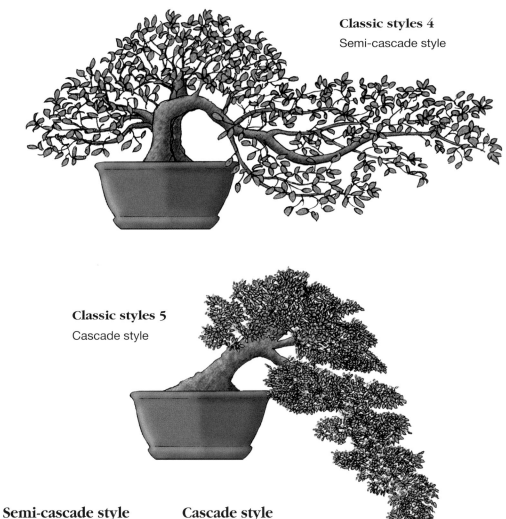

Classic styles 4
Semi-cascade style

Classic styles 5
Cascade style

Semi-cascade style

This style represents a tree growing on a cliff face. The trunk should fall below the rim of the pot but not below the base of the pot. In order to comply with classic bonsai rules, there must be a crown of foliage directly above the base of the trunk.

Cascade style

This also depicts a tree growing on a cliff face, but the trunk falls below the base of the pot. To comply with classic rules, there must be a crown of foliage above the base of the trunk, and the lowest point must be directly below the base of the trunk.

Classic styles 6

Broom style

Classic styles 7

The raft style is similar to the forest style, but the trunks are in fact the branches of a buried trunk.

Broom style

This style is based on the natural habit of the zelkova tree. The trunk is straight and free of branches. A number of branches radiate from the top of the trunk in all directions. These branches divide at regular intervals to produce a domed, twiggy canopy.

Forest style

As the name suggests, the forest style consists of multiple trunks of different heights and thicknesses but of a similar character. The largest trunks should be planted toward the front of the composition to create perspective.

What plants?

Choosing the right species

The simple rule is to select plants that you know do well in the environment you intend to provide for them. If you intend to keep your bonsai outside, any hardy native or garden species will do — in theory. In practice it's not quite so simple. The same applies to indoor bonsai: any woody species that lives happily in your home could be used.

The Chinese juniper makes an excellent bonsai plant, as this cascade-style specimen shows.

In practice, not all species are happy living in small containers. Eucalypts and hebes are notorious haters of root confinement, and refuse to produce a potful of fine roots, no matter what you do. Also, bonsai look better with foliage that is small in proportion to the tree. Although leaf size will reduce dramatically with bonsai training, and regular pinching and pruning (less so on tropical and subtropical species), there is a limit, which varies between species. Large-leaved species such as the edible fig or horse chestnut will never produce leaves

The Japanese maple with its brilliant red autumn colours is one of the traditional bonsai species.

small enough to look right on a bonsai. On the other hand, if you use dwarf fig varieties or cotoneaster, for example, you will already have small leaves before you start.

It's wise to focus on species that have already been tried and tested before venturing into exotics. When you stumble across that wonderful red-leaved, compact little whatnot that you can imagine would look beautiful as a bonsai, consider whether anyone has tried it before,

and if you haven't yet seen a bonsai whatnot, it's probably because whatnots aren't really suitable.

It's difficult to recommend a list of tropical or subtropical species to use for making your own bonsai. The traditional subjects are not usually sold as ordinary houseplants. The species available for indoor cultivation are also variable, being subject to the whims and economic pressures of the industry.

However, it is easy to recommend a list of hardy species that are readily available — whether in garden centres, in your garden or in the countryside around you. The table includes some of the most trees and shrubs that are most suitable for growing as outdoor bonsai.

Hawthorn is one of our native countryside plants that makes an ideal candidate for bonsai.

Hardy plants suitable for bonsai

Garden plants	Countryside plants
Cotoneaster	Elm (*Ulmus*)
Juniper (*Juniperus*)	Hawthorn (*Crataegus*)
Dwarf spruce (*Picea* varieties)	Field maple (*Acer campestre*)
Dwarf pine (but not *Pinus mugo* 'Mops')	Pine (*Pinus*)
Japanese quince (*Chaenomeles japonica*)	Larch (*Larix*)
	Birch (*Betula*)
Japanese maple (*Acer palmatum*)	Yew (*Taxus*)
Privet (*Ligustrum*)	
Some crab apples (*Malus* species and varieties)	

This alder has been grown according to one of the non-classical styles — namely the clump style.

What to look for

There's more to choosing a plant to train as a bonsai than selecting an appropriate species. You need to examine the plant closely, looking at various aspects and trying to imagine how they would fit into a bonsai image.

For example, plant breeders have produced varieties of some species that have contorted or spiralled branches and trunks. At first sight, these appear ideal for bonsai — until you discover that the leaves are enormous, the internodes are long and the branches have minds of their own!

Exotic, brightly coloured or flamboyant varieties seldom make good bonsai. A bonsai is a miniature image of a tree — real or fantastic — and anything that detracts from or overpowers that image will spoil the bonsai. Keep to species with simple growth habits and foliage.

Also, it would be a good idea to aim at a more traditional, tree-like image for your first few attempts at growing your own bonsai, rather than breaking the rules before you have mastered them.

Once you have chosen your species, it remains to decide which specimen to choose from 30 or 40 display plants.

Start by looking at the surface roots. 'What surface roots?' you ask, because you won't see any. Garden centre plants are usually planted deep in the pots to reduce the risk of the roots drying out after potting. Ignore the stares and remarks of other customers, and poke around in the soil at the base of the trunks feeling for thick roots. Whenever you find a plant that has reasonably evenly distributed thick roots at a similar level, put it to one side and ignore the rest.

Now examine the trunks of all the plants you have put to one side. Bear in mind that what appears to be the trunk (or at least the most dominant growth line) at the moment would not necessarily be the trunk in the final design. Perhaps you could remove the top of the plant and use just the first or second branch to make a new trunk line. On the other hand, you may be able to cut the top off a ten-foot high

This trident maple possesses a particularly good trunk base.

hornbeam and grow an entire new set of branches on the 18-inch tall stump.

Don't assume that the angle at which the tree is currently planted is permanent. You may discover that if you tilt the plant one way or another,

entirely new and more exciting possibilities become clear. Take your time, because nothing is more likely to dampen your bonsai spirits than having your first potential masterpiece turn out to be a dog's breakfast!

By the time you have narrowed down your choice of plants by studying the roots and trunk lines, you will probably only have a few remaining. Now look at the existing branches and try to decide whether you can work with them. Don't try to work out an on-the-spot design, just see if the branches are reasonably well placed and flexible. With broadleaved species, hardy or otherwise, you can usually cut all the branches off and start over, but on conifers that isn't possible, so you have no choice but to use whatever branches already exist.

Just one more piece of advice: don't go overboard and buy every interesting plant you

A crab apple bonsai looks very attractive whether in blossom or in fruit.

find. There are so many new bonsai enthusiasts who proudly announce that they have so many hundred 'bonsai'. 'Well,' they qualify, 'plants rather than actual bonsai at the moment.' And that's the problem. If you accumulate too many plants, none of them receive the attention they deserve. You spend so much time watering, feeding and generally fiddling with them all that you never actually get round to making a bonsai with any of them. Creating a bonsai requires focus and careful consideration, so concentrate on one plant at a time.

Where to begin

The first (and possibly the most important) thing to consider is the type of tree you're dealing with, because there are a considerable differences in the way in which various species grow, both in nature and in a container.

Coniferous or deciduous?

Think of an ancient pine tree with its tall, straight trunk and sparse, cascading branches. The crown is a shallow dome, possibly slightly pointed, and there are large spaces between the 'clouds' of foliage. Now imagine an ancient oak — a wide, dense dome supported by a relatively short, thick trunk, and with little or no discernible space between individual foliage clouds. The branches on the oak begin by ascending and soon arch over to become horizontal, with the outermost branchlets spread wide to fill all the available spaces.

It's no coincidence that virtually all temperate and most tropical and subtropical trees follow one of these basic growth habits. The final form of any tree is genetically programmed and has its key in the way the buds are carried on the growing shoots. A brand new seedling has all the information you need to tell you what the tree's growth habit will be for the next couple of centuries.

*The best bonsai are created by working with the tree's natural growth patterns, as is shown by these two specimens, grown in non-classical styles: (**below**) a hemlock (windswept style) and (**right**) a Japanese maple (clump style).*

Within each of these two basic tree forms, the variations are endless. But the distinction between conifers and deciduous broadleaved trees will always be clear. Even when a tree has been battered by all the inclement weather and misfortunes that nature can throw at it in the most inhospitable of environments, the pre-determined growth pattern will be the overriding factor influencing its structure.

These are the two basic upright tree forms in their most simple state, and it would be a

Another bonsai in a non-classical style — a sabina juniper grown in the driftwood style.

good idea to master these before progressing to more adventurous styles — provided, of course, that your raw material allows you to do so.

Analysing your material

There is absolutely nothing to be gained by trying to force a plant to grow in a way that is entirely unnatural for that particular species.

If, for example, you have a prostrate juniper, whose natural habit is to grow flat along the ground, trying to force it into a tall, formal upright bonsai style will always lead to disappointment. The plant will simply refuse to co-

operate. The top will become weak and probably eventually die, while the lower branches will become more dominant.

On the other hand, if you have a strongly upward-growing plant, such as one of the columnar cypresses, it will refuse point blank to be trained in a cascade or semi-cascade style. The lower parts will either constantly bend upward, regardless of how often they are wired down, or they will weaken and die. No matter how hard you pinch and prune the top, it will always be the most dominant part of the plant.

When you buy plants from a garden centre, the label should

Broadleaved trees such as this silver birch planted with a Japanese maple take much longer to shape than conifers but offer more choice in terms of style.

tell you what the growth habit is. If you're digging a plant from the garden, its natural habit should already be obvious. To make your life easier at first, it would be a good idea to avoid either strongly vertical or prostrate species — unless, of course, you particularly want a tall upright or cascading bonsai.

Working with your plant

Another important distinction between coniferous and broadleaved species is that, in general, broadleaved species can be cut back to bare branches, or even a branchless trunk, and they will sprout new shoots for training and development. This is never the case with conifers: if you eliminate all the foliage on a conifer branch, that branch will die.

This doesn't mean that conifers are necessarily more difficult or demanding. On the contrary, conifers generally have such dense foliage, and such a profusion of branches and shoots, that you can very often produce an almost complete bonsai image in a single session. On the other hand, you have no choice but to work with the existing branches, which makes designing your bonsai a *re*-active process.

Conversely, designing broad-leaved bonsai is a more *pro*-active process. You can decide in advance what style you want and roughly where you want the branches to grow, and set about achieving that. If you change your mind, you can cut everything off and start again.

The time factor also differs between the two types of plant. Whereas conifers can often be shaped into a bonsai image in a single session, this is extremely unlikely with a broadleaved plant. At best, you

might be able to arrange branches into a basic skeletal structure, but there will always be several years' work needed before it is more or less complete. To compensate for the extra time and effort needed to develop a deciduous broad-leaved bonsai, you will be rewarded by the spectacular autumn colours, the stark tracery of twigs in winter and the dainty, brightly coloured new leaves that appear as the tree wakes from its winter slumber.

Jins and sharis

Deadwood features can play an important role in the design of coniferous bonsai. Such features are common in nature on conifers but only very rarely occur in broadleaved trees — so rarely in fact that they are virtually never used on broadleaved bonsai.

On a coniferous bonsai, such features make the tree appear older. They tell a story of how the tree used to be and how it has suffered at the hands of mother nature. Perhaps a lightening strike, or the ravages of strong winds have killed parts of the tree. Perhaps years of drought or attack by pests or disease were the cause. Almost all ancient conifers in nature will have some deadwood features, regardless of whether they are growing in the high mountains or in the peaceful valleys below. Some, especially old junipers, can be almost all deadwood, with only one or two narrow living veins connecting the roots to the foliage.

Some people think that creating jins and sharis on a bonsai is cruel, but doing so merely accelerates what the tree would almost certainly do of its own accord before too long. The advantage of creating your own deadwood areas, rather than waiting for the tree to make up its mind, is that you can control the exact size, shape and location, thus incorporating the deadwood in the overall design.

Deadwood features on coniferous bonsai simply mimic the development of such trees in the wild. This is especially true of junipers, as these two fine specimens show.

Jins

A jin is the remains of a branch that has died. The bark has peeled and the wood has become etched and bleached by the elements. Jins may be short stubs dotted around the trunk or they may be entire branches. Perhaps the top of the tree has died, leaving an apical jin pointing skyward like a skeletal finger.

Jins are a useful way of adding the impression of age to an otherwise young-looking bonsai. They are also extremely useful when it comes to disguising the fact that unwanted branches have recently been removed. Apical jins are even more handy because they enable you to reduce a tall, leggy conifer to more bonsai-like proportions. They can be whittled and carved to imitate the texture of old exposed wood battered by the elements.

Sharis

A shari is an area of trunk that has died and lost its bark. In tall-growing conifers this could be the result of a lightning strike, disease or a branch that has fallen and ripped the bark from the trunk as it fell.

Like jins, sharis are the norm on junipers of all types. Junipers have a natural way of balancing the foliage mass with the roots' ability to supply it with water and nutrients. In response to adverse conditions such as drought, heat, disturbance or even just overgrown foliage, they will readily shed branches. Since the tissue connecting the roots with the branches in junipers is less able to redirect itself, the roots that fed shed branches will also die, and so will the tissue between them.

Making a jin 1

To make a jin, first prune the branch to a little longer than the desired jin, cut a line through the bark around the base of the branch, then squeeze off the bark with pliers.

line cut
through
bark

Making jins

To make a jin, cut the branch to about one-and-a-half times as long as you wish the final jin to be (if it ends up too long, you can easily shorten it later). Then cut a vertical 'eye' shape through the bark around the base of the branch. The purpose of this is to allow the bark to heal without encroaching on the jin itself.

Now take a pair of pliers and gently squeeze the bark all along the cut branch. You'll see how this separates the bark from the wood, and the bark will peel away easily. This works best when the tree is actively growing and the sap is flowing well. In autumn and winter, the bark becomes more firmly fixed to the wood and the squeezing technique doesn't work anywhere near so well. In this case, you will have to resort to scraping the bark away with a blade.

Having removed all traces of bark, you can now shape the jin. Natural jins tend to be slightly pointed because the fractured end grain will decay or erode more rapidly than the sides But whatever you do, avoid just sharpening the jin like a pencil — this looks really artificial. On larger jins you could use an electric carving tool, but these also leave an unnatural finish unless used by an expert.

By far the best way to shape a jin is to crush the end with pliers and then peel back slivers of wood to expose the grain. You will find that the slivers get thinner as they near the trunk. If you do this with patience and care, the result will be an entirely natural-looking jin, which is hardly surprising since all you have done is what nature would do on a larger scale.

Making a jin 2

Peel away layers of wood to shape the jin and to create a natural texture.

Making a shari

First cut an outline with a sharp modelling knife, then carefully peel the bark away. Wide sharis are best made in stages to minimise the trauma to the tree.

Making sharis

Sharis should be made with care, since they expose a great deal of wood. Spring and early summer are the best times for this operation. Always make sure you leave at least two-thirds of the bark intact and that the shari doesn't spiral around the trunk, cutting off the sap flow to living branches.

First mark the desired edges of the shari with a felt-tip pen, then cut through the bark just inside this line. Stop the shari a fraction above the soil, so that it doesn't become permanently wet and begin to rot. Peel the bark between the cuts and seal the edges with cut paste.

Next year, examine the edges to see if the healing callus is visible. If not, you can peel back more bark until you find live tissue. If you can see the callus and it looks nice and plump, then you can cut back to the line you marked the year before.

This staggered approach provides a fail-safe to reduce the risk of doing too much damage to the tree in one go.

Preserving deadwood

In nature, deadwood becomes bleached by the sun to develop a beautiful silvery-white patina. This can be imitated effectively with a solution of lime sulphur, while at the same time the wood is preserved. Lime sulphur used to be available in garden centres as a winter fungicide, but it has long been superseded by more effective chemicals. Nowadays, bonsai nurseries are the only places you'll be able to find it.

The very smelly, yellow liquid is painted on the dead wood and allowed to dry. As it dries it becomes almost pure white. However, after a few weeks the harshness of the white becomes subdued and a more natural colour develops.

Lime sulphur should be applied at least once, or preferably twice, a year. The wood gradually becomes impregnated with lime and develops a hard 'crust' that will last for many years. Some Japanese bonsai have jins and sharis that have been preserved for generations using nothing but lime sulphur.

Glossary

Adventitious: a word describing buds that appear spontaneously on old branches

Akadama: a Japanese growing medium — particles of clay-like material that retain their structure when wet

Annealed: a word that describes (copper) wire that has been temporarily softened with heat

Anodised: describes (aluminium) wire that has been coloured brown to match the bark

Apex: the top of a tree or the tip of a shoot — hence the term **apical,** describing growth at one of these points

Axil: the angle between the petiole (leaf stalk) and the stem of a plant — hence **axillary,** describing growth from this point

Bunjingi: literati style — a bonsai style not described in this book

Calcifuge: a plant that will not tolerate calcium (lime) in the soil

Calcined clay: clay that has been baked to form stable granules

Cambium: the layer between the bark and the wood, responsible for all growth

Chokkan: formal upright style

Cut paste: a commercial product for sealing pruning wounds

Deciduous: describes a tree that loses all its leaves in autumn

Ericaceous soil: calcium-free soil

Evergreen: describes a tree that retains green leaves all year round

Fukinagashi: windswept style (see page 68)

Grit: mineral particles used in soil and measuring 2–4 mm in diameter

Han-kengai: semi-cascade style

Hardy: able to withstand freezing

Hoki-dachi: broom style

Ikadabuki: raft style

Ishitzuke: root-over-rock style (see page 6)

Jin: a dead branch, stripped of its bark

Kabudachi: clump style (see page 65)

Kanuma: a Japanese growing medium for azaleas

Kengai: cascade style

Lenticel: a pore on the stem, used for exchange of gases

Lime sulphur: a compound used for bleaching and preserving jins and sharis

Medullary ray: a channel within the heartwood used for storage of sugars while the plant is dormant

Moyogi: informal upright style

Mycorrhiza: a fungus that lives in a symbiotic relationship with a tree, whereby the tree supplies sugars to the fungus while the fungus gathers water and minerals for the tree

Nebari: visible surface roots

Netsunanari: exposed root style — a bonsai style not described in this book

NPK: formula indicating the composition of fertilisers (N = nitrogen, P = phosphate, K = potassium)

Osmosis: the process whereby water and nutrients are absorbed by the roots

Pathogen: a harmful organism, usually causing disease

Penjing: Chinese bonsai

Petiole: leaf stalk

Phloem: the layer beneath the bark but outside the cambium (see above) and responsible for transporting sugars from the leaves to other parts of the tree

Photosynthesis: the process whereby sugars are manufactured in the leaves, using water, carbon dioxide from the air, and sunlight

Root hair: a single-cell protrusion from a root — the main means of absorbing water and nutrients

Saikei: bonsai landscape in a tray

Sapwood: see **xylem**

Shari: an area of a trunk or branch that has been stripped of its bark

Sharimiki: driftwood style (see page 70)

Stomata: a 'breathing' pore on the underside (usually) of a leaf

Subtropical: when applied to plants, means they can tolerate low temperatures but not total freezing

Tropical: term used to describe plants that cannot tolerate low temperatures

Xylem: the outer layers of wood responsible for transporting water from the roots to all parts of the tree

Yamadori: a wild plant used for bonsai

Yose-ue: forest style

The trident maple is an excellent candidate for bonsai and is also very tolerant of the polluted air that predominates in urban environments.

Learning more

Bonsai courses

By far the best way to learn about bonsai is to attend classes with a good teacher. Most specialist bonsai nurseries will offer courses at all levels — and if not, they should be able to recommend someone.

Bonsai clubs

Getting into contact with other bonsai enthusiasts by joining a club is also an excellent way to learn. Bonsai lovers are always eager to pass on their knowledge to others. Because bonsai clubs are run by enthusiasts in their spare time, the contact addresses frequently change, so it would not be helpful to list them here. Ask at your local library or horticultural society.

Bonsai magazines

There are a number of specialist magazines published, but unfortunately none are available through newsagents. Your nearest bonsai nursery should be able to give you subscription details.

The Internet

These days, the Internet provides an amazing resource for bonsai information. A good place to start is the Bonsai Web Ring, which includes hundreds of bonsai-related websites that have been quality-tested before inclusion. You can find it at **http://www.webring.org/cgi-bin/ webring?ring=bunjin&home**.

Another excellent resource for bonsai growers is the Internet Bonsai Club, which can be found at **http://www.internetbonsaiclub.org**. This is an e-mail-based newsgroup where members exchange advice and observations.

Many clubs and national organisations have websites that can be easily located through any search engine.

Index